Honor &

By Garry Bowles and Ed Polonitza

Prelude

I have eaten your bread and salt,
I have drunk your water and wine;
The deaths ye died I have watched beside,
And the lives ye lead were mine.

Was there aught that I did not share
In vigil or toil or ease ---
One joy or woe that I did not know
Dear hearts across the seas?

I have written the tale of our life
For a sheltered peoples mirth,
In jesting guise --- but ye are wise,
And ye know what the jest is worth

---Rudyard Kipling

Table of Contents

Honor & Courage
The History of the 8th Cavalry Regiment

Published by Kensington Pond Books
Copyright (c) 2006 by Garry Bowles and Ed Polonitza

Cover Design by Garry Bowles and George Cook

Book editing and design by Donna L. Ferrier, Ada, Oklahoma

Library of Congress Catalog Card Number
applied for March 2006

ISBN# 978-1-4116-8354-9

First Edition: March 2006
Printed in the United States of America

HONOR & COURAGE

The History of the 8th Cavalry Regiment

On July 28, 1866, Colonel John I. Gregg stood in front of the troops of the 8th Cavalry Regiment at Angel Island, California, in honor of the initial formation of the United States Army's newest unit of horse cavalry. In his address to the regiment's troops, Colonel Gregg noted that the cavalryman's first goal was to defend the country against its enemies by fighting with "Honor and Courage." Today, 140 years later, Colonel Gregg's charge to his soldiers is preserved in the unit crest of the 8th Cavalry. Recognizing its heritage as a horse cavalry regiment, the distinctive insignia of the 8th Cavalry includes a horse charging into battle over the words, "Honor and Courage."

Pony Patrol American Frontier

Throughout its long and distinguished history, the 8th Cavalry has been true to those words of its first commanding officer. Its initial mission was tied directly to America's "Manifest Destiny," as the unit escorted settlers, opened trade routes, and fought Indians in the American Northwest. The 8th Cavalry served with distinction in the Spanish American War and during the occupation of the Philippines in the early part of the last century.

On September 13, 1921, the 8th Cavalry Regiment was assigned to the 1st Cavalry Division stationed at Fort Bliss, Texas. On the eve of World War II, the 8th Cavalry turned in its horses and was reorganized as an armored unit. Fighting as part of the famed 1st Cav, the regiment distinguished itself in World War II leading the army's attack across the Pacific into the Japanese homeland. General Douglas Macarthur gave the 1st Cavalry Division its nickname, "The First Team" in honor of its exploits. The 8th Cavalry shared in the distinction of being "First in Manila" and "First in Tokyo."

After serving as an occupation force in Japan in the aftermath of World War II, the 8th Cavalry was once again called to battle. When the armies of North Korea swarmed across the 38th parallel into the South, the 1st Cavalry Division was thrown in front of the Communist onslaught. The cavalrymen were successful in pushing the invaders back across the 38th parallel, and on October 18, 1950, achieved another first---"First in Pyongyang," the North Korean capital. The troopers of the 8th Cavalry spent the next several years battling the North Korean and Chinese armies as the conflict flowed back and forth across the 38th parallel. Although the Korean War officially ended in July 1953, the 8th Cavalry remained in Korea until the early summer of 1965.

The 8th Cavalry would again be ordered into combat. This time, the 8th Cavalry and the 1st Cavalry Division would return to their roots as true cavalry units. But instead of riding horses into battle, the troopers of the 8th Cavalry would ride helicopters. The colors of the 8th Cavalry were returned from Korea, and on July 1, 1965, during a cere-

First team bayonet charge on the Japanese-occupied
island of New Guinea

8th Cavalry takes "Old Baldy" hill 272

mony at Fort Benning, Georgia, the 1st Battalion (Airborne), 511th Infantry became the 2nd Battalion (Airborne) of the 8th Cavalry. For a brief period of time, the 8th Cavalry was manned by proud paratroopers who would lead the unit into some of the bloodiest combat of the Vietnam War. The 8th Cavalry fought with distinction for more than seven years in Vietnam and participated in all of the war's major campaigns.

With the exception of the brief predeployment period in 1965, the 8th Cavalry had been overseas for more than 30 years when the unit returned from Vietnam to Fort Hood, Texas, in 1972. Fourteen of these 30-plus years were spent in combat, fighting relentless and dangerous enemies. At Fort Hood, the 8th Cavalry went through another transformation, becoming the Army's premier heavy-armored division. The soldiers of the 8th Cavalry have continued to serve with distinction in Desert Storm, as peacekeepers in the Balkans, and most recently, in Iraq.

During its 140-year history, the 8th Cavalry has charged into battle as horse cavalry, light armor, parachute infantry, airmobile infantry, and heavy armor. But one common thread has united the cavalrymen who have worn its colors. From the frontiers of the Old West, to the

Vietnam paratrooper patrol

Philippine jungles, across the Pacific, into the frozen hills of Korea and the swamps and rice paddies of Vietnam, and across the desert battlefields of the Middle East, all have fought with honor and courage. Thus, the troopers of the 8th Cavalry title the chronicle of their experiences in recognition of those who came before them and those who will fight under the colors of this distinguished unit in future battles.

Dedication

O ne little known aspect of modern warfare is that few of the soldiers deployed into combat operations have ever fired a shot in anger. In fact, many never heard a shot fired in anger. This is certainly true of the Vietnam War. For every grunt who spent his year beating the bush and coming eyeball to eyeball with the Viet Cong and North Vietnamese infantry there were a dozen doing rear echelon jobs.

Light Infantry

Honor and Courage is a story about a parachute infantry company that was at the tip of the Air Cav spear during its year in combat in South Vietnam. The infantry company was the focal point of the army's effort throughout the war. Due to the nature of the strategy and tactics used it was the norm for rifle company to conduct operations on its own and only rarely would units above the company level maneuver as a single entity. An outfit such as Alpha Company, 2nd Battalion (Airborne) 8th Cavalry although organized as light infantry could bring a fearsome array of firepower upon any enemy force.

TO&E

The table of organization and equipment or TO&E defines the structure, personnel strength and equipment of an American military unit.The TO&E for Alpha Company called for 6 officers and 168 enlisted men. While this was its authorized strength, it was rare for us to deploy to the field at full strength. Soldiers were needed for various rear area tasks and stayed behind at the An Khe base camp. Others had been evacuated due to wounds or disease. Almost every operation saw Alpha Company soldiers killed in action. As the unit's year in Vietnam progressed, some of the original members of the company saw their enlistments end and shipped stateside for discharge. The stream of replacements never kept up with the attrition. So it was not unusual for A Company to deploy on a combat operation with no more than 100 of its 174 man authorized strength.

Ticket Punching

Rifle companies are commanded by captains. When the 1st Cavalry Division deployed to Vietnam, its company commanders were experienced officers with six or more years army service. As the war progressed such officers became less available and the quality and skills at this level of leadership deteriorated as the war evolved. A standard policy, which created havoc and disruption at the combat level, was the idea of "ticket punching". It was considered career suicide for an infantry officer not to have command experience in combat. A career officer needed that ticket punched in order to move up the ladder to the next level of command. The Army viewed this, perhaps incorrectly, as a good way to develop a strong cadre of trained combat leaders. As a result, Alpha Company had a half a dozen company commanders during its initial year in combat and three battalion commanders. Just as they begin to acquire competence through experience they would be replaced by someone else needing their ticket punched.

Assault Into An Lao (c)
Illustrated by George Cook

Follow Me

Alpha Company consisted of a small headquarters element, three rifle platoons and a weapons platoon. The rifle platoons had an authorized strength of one officer and forty-three enlisted soldiers. The officer was a lieutenant, generally with two to three years' military service. He would be the first officer that the enlisted men would encounter in the chain of command. The motto of the infantry is "Follow Me" and this lieutenant was the poster boy for this motto. He led by example and experienced the same dangers and hardships as the enlisted soldiers he led. Being an infantry lieutenant in Vietnam was as dangerous a job as there was.

Sergeants, Squads, & Soldiers

The young platoon leader was assisted by a platoon sergeant who was a senior enlisted man. For Alpha Company these platoon sergeants were experienced and capable leaders many of whom had Korean War or even World War II combat service under their belts. Each of A Company's three rifle platoons was organized into three rifle squads and a weapons squad. The rifle squads were led by a staff sergeant and included two fire teams with a team leader, an automatic rifleman, one or two riflemen, and a grenadier. The automatic rifleman and the rifleman were armed with the M16 rifle. This weapon is still in service today. It fires a 5.56-millimeter round (.223 caliber) and is capable of a heavy volume of accurate fire. Although there was an organizational distinction between the rifleman and the automatic rifleman, there was no difference between these jobs since every M16 had the capability for semi-automatic or automatic fire. A quick flick of the selector switch on the side of the weapon allowed you to choose your rate of fire.

Direct Fire

The rifle platoon grenadiers were armed with the M79 grenade launcher, which was capable of firing a 40-millimeter grenade at ranges well in front of the platoon position. This weapon gave the rifle platoon the capability of projecting a high explosive round with effective killing radius into an enemy positions and bunkers.

The weapons squad of each rifle platoon was authorized 12 men whose principal armament consisted of two M60 machine guns and two 90-millimeter anti-tank weapons. As Alpha Company soon discovered that these anti-tank weapons were too heavy to be carried through the jungles of the Central Highlands they were left in base camp and replaced by the LAW, a lightweight disposable shoulder fired rocket. The 90-millimeter gunners were used to fill vacant slots in the various platoons. The M60 machine gun fired the NATO 7.62 round and was a formidable weapon and used very effectively to break up enemy assaults into the platoon's ranks.

Indirect Fire

Alpha Company's Weapons Platoon included three 81-millimeter mortars capable of firing high explosive, white phosphorous and illumination rounds at ranges up to five thousand meters. These mortars gave the company a very effective indirect fire capability, which could wreak havoc on an enemy formation. Any member of a mortar crew still recalls humping their 98-pound mortars through the jungle and up and down the hills we crossed. The burden of the platoon ammo bearers was even worse. Each ammo bearer would carry a backpack loaded with five or six mortar rounds weighing fifteen pounds each. Although heavy and cumbersome we were very happy to have our mortars available to bang out round after round at enemy positions we encountered.

So this was Alpha Company. Not only were we well equipped and armed, but perhaps most importantly each of us was a graduate of the army parachute training school at Fort Benning, Georgia. Jump training and the esprit we felt as being part of the heroic paratrooper tradition gave every Alpha Airborne Warrior the confidence that we were more than a match for the enemy we would encounter during our year in combat.

Their 365-Day War

Honor & Courage is dedicated to all the soldiers of the 1st Air Cavalry Division who fought America's longest war on foreign soil. The Air Cavalry advance party arrived in July 1965 and was the vanguard of the first division-sized unit deployed to Vietnam. Year after year for seven years, troopers of the Air Cavalry arrived "in country" to fight their 365-day war. In 1972, when America wound down its involvement in Vietnam, 1st Air Cavalry units were amongst the last to furl their colors and return stateside. Any trooper who served a tour in Vietnam with the Air Cav will tell you, "I don't know who lost that war, because when I left, we were winning!"

Bound for War

On August 20, 1965, 169 troopers of 2nd Battalion (Airborne) 8th Cavalry boarded the USNS *Geiger* in Savannah, Georgia, for their voyage to Vietnam. The *Geiger* docked at the port city of Qui Nhon Republic of South Vietnam on September 21 after 31 days at sea. The next day the men of A Company were transported by Chinooks to Camp Radcliff, the Air Cavalry base camp at An Khe.

I
"Cavalry...
And I Don't Mean Horses"

*I*n a May 1954 *Harper's* magazine article entitled, "Calvary...and I Don't Mean Horses," Major General James Gavin of World War II paratrooper fame introduced the concept of air mobility. In one paragraph he summed it up in a nutshell:

"Jump Off"
Illustrated By George Cook

"Where was the Cavalry?...and I don't mean horses. I mean helicopters and light aircraft, to lift soldiers armed with automatic weapons and hand-carried light anti-tank weapons, and also lightweight reconnaissance vehicles, mounting anti-tank weapons equal or better than the Russian T-34s...If ever in the history of our armed forces there was a need for the cavalry arm---airlifted in light planes, helicopters, and assault-type aircraft---this was it...Only by exploiting to the utmost the great potential of flight can we combine complete dispersion in the defense with the facility of rapidly massing for the counter-attack which today's and tomorrow's Army must possess."

A decade after Major General Gavin wrote that prophetic article, Sergeant Art Miller and his fellow paratroopers of A Company, 511th Airborne Infantry, 11th Air Assault Division (Test), were making military history, as they trained with soldiers of the 2nd Infantry Division in the pine barrens of Fort Benning, Georgia. The history they were making combined the swift mobility of the old-fashioned horse cavalry with the lethal firepower of a modern Army division.

Major General Gavin's vision, along with an odd-looking flying machine, nicknamed the "Huey," had evolved into a revolutionary new military doctrine called "airmobility," a unit like no other. Air mobility

Sergeant Arthur Miller

would free the Army from the tyranny of terrain, and Gavin's dream of troopers being able to swiftly attack enemy positions using air-assault tactics would become a reality. On July 1, 1965, the 11th Air Assault and elements of the 2nd Infantry Division, were redesignated the 1st Cavalry Division (Airmobile). Sergeant Miller was now a member of A Company, 2nd Battalion (Airborne), 8th Cavalry, of the 1st Cavalry Division (Airmobile).

On July 28, 1965, President Lyndon B. Johnson, on a nationally tele-vised news conference, announced to America, "I have today ordered to Vietnam the Airmobile Division." Within a few weeks, Sergeant Miller and his buddies would be boarding troop transports for deployment to the Republic of South Vietnam and to war.

Specialist Juan Fernandez, a rifleman with the 3rd Platoon, recalls, "Reveille was at 0300 hours that morning, and as we marched from our barracks, I remembered how pitch black it was. We lined up in platoon formation with all our gear and waited for the buses that would take us to Savannah where we would board our troop transport, the USNS *Geiger*. After a several-hour bus trip, we arrived at dockside; some of the battalion had arrived earlier and were in the process of walking up the gangplank in single file, duffle bags on their shoulders. According to the morning report and roster typed by the company clerk, Specialist 4th Class Billie Brandenburg, a total of 169 officers and men of A Company boarded the ship that day. It took the entire day for the battalion to board, and we set sail for Vietnam on the evening of August 20, 1965.

On August 25, I celebrated my 18th birthday aboard the *Geiger*, as we steamed through the Panama Canal. We spent our days aboard the ship in a fairly predictable routine. A lot of time was spent standing in line waiting to get into the mess hall, with an equal amount of time spent standing in line waiting

3rd Platoon, A Company
511th Airborne

for a turn in the latrine. In between standing in lines, we had lots of physical training and classes on combat tactics and even had several opportunities to fire our weapons at targets towed from the stern of the ship. On September 5, we docked at Pearl Harbor, and the entire platoon was able to take a much-appreciated shore leave. It was great to be on dry land, if only for a few hours. The day after leaving Hawaii we were told we had a new company commander, Captain Roger L. McElroy, who had replaced Captain Tom Forman, our very popular CO.

Apparently, Captain Forman had enjoyed his shore leave too much and had been involved in a barroom brawl, and much to the dismay of most of A Company, had been relieved of his command. The voyage continued without further incident until September 13, when we ran into

USNS Geiger

Shore Leave in Hawaii

some rough weather and spent several days being tossed about by a typhoon. We arrived at the island of Guam on September 16, and, once again, we were able to leave the boat and stretch our legs before continuing on to Vietnam. My favorite memory of the voyage was the time I spent standing at the front of the ship and watching the dolphins and flying fish swim and fly through the big waves created by the *Geiger's* bow. It was a wonderful thing to watch."

On September 21, 1965, after 31 days at sea, the USNS *Geiger* dropped anchor off the port city of Qui Nhon, Republic of South Vietnam. The troopers of A Company were issued a combat load of ammunition and climbed aboard World War II-type landing craft for the short ride to the beach.

"I remember the heat," recalls trooper Specialist Bill Garlinger. "It must have been 110 degrees. We landed without incident, and we were

Heavy equipment arrived by LST

all sort of milling about, very curious about everything. There was a large group of Vietnamese workers loading stuff on trucks, and a trooper next to me said that he was glad that they had issued us ammo with all the Vietnamese on the beach. I turned to him and said that they were friendlies; they were on our side. The soldier smiled, and asked me how I could tell. I was suddenly glad I was carrying a loaded M-16." That night Specialist Bill Garlinger and the soldiers of Alpha Company made camp on the tarmac at Qui Nhon airstrip.

The next morning after a breakfast of c-rations, they loaded into Chinook transport helicopters for the final leg of their journey to the small South Vietnamese village of An Khe in the central highlands of Vietnam. This is where the new 1st Air Cav base camp was located, astride a major infiltration route of the North Vietnamese Army (NVA). When the 1st Cavalry's advance party arrived in August 1965, it took operational control of a large parcel

Troopers coming ashore at Qui Nhon Vietnam

of land at the base of Hon Cong Mountain next to An Khe. The advance party stripped to the waist, and in the best "can do" tradition of the U.S. Army, started to carve from the jungle with machetes and chainsaws what was to become one of the most important military installations in the world.

The base camp housed up to 20,000 soldiers and provided facilities and servicing to more than 500 helicopters and 100 fixed-wing aircraft of various sizes, shapes, and nomenclature. The airfield complex was called the "Golf Course," so named because when the advance party arrived, the leader of the group, Brigadier General John M. Wright, announced that they were about to construct the world's largest helipad, which had to be as flat and smooth as a Golf Course. The General addressed his men, "Gentlemen," he began, "you will all be issued a machete or a grub hook; they both do exactly the same job. We are going to cut brush until we have a Golf Course here. You might as well hang your rank insignia on a tree because, until this area is transformed, we will all avail ourselves to this manual task. When the Golf Course is complete you may then put back your rank insignia." General Wright was a World War II veteran and a strong advocate of leading by example. He then tied a bandana around his forehead, stripped off his fatigue blouse, took his machete, and started to make large bushes into small bushes. The General had learned brush-clearing two decades earlier under the harsh tutelage of the Japanese Army as a prisoner of war. When the Air Cav arrived in September and moved inland to the base camp, those arriving in choppers found a landing field that was as smooth and as flat as a Golf Course. The Air Cav now had a home for its hundreds of helicopters and planes. The "Greenline," a 17-mile

defensive perimeter that snaked around the base camp, protected those aircraft and base complex from any and all enemy attacks.

The base camp was named Camp Radcliff in honor of Major Donald Radcliff, who was the first trooper killed in the 1st Cavalry Division. Major Radcliff was the Executive

Boarding the Chinooks for the flight to An Khe

Officer (XO) of the 1st Squadron, 9th Cavalry, and was posthumously awarded the Distinguished Flying Cross for his actions in combat against the enemy. He had arrived with the advance party and had been a member of the site selection committee, who was responsible for scouring the countryside for the best possible location for the Air Cavalry base camp.

On August 18, the advance party's commo team picked up radio traffic indicating a Marine combat unit was short of assault choppers. Major Radcliff volunteered to fly in support of the Marines and was killed while providing covering fire to the lift ships landing Marines at a hot landing zone (LZ). His gallant actions saved countless lives and enabled the Marine lift ships to land safely. The NVA gunners directed intense fire at his helicopter, and the young officer was mortally wounded, as bullets tore through his gunship. The 37-year-old major died at the controls of his chopper during his baptism of fire. It would be from there that the young troopers of A Company would begin their war.

II
1st Brigade, First to Fight

1st Airborne Brigade moves to Pleiku

The 1st Airborne Brigade's deployment to Vietnam in August 1965 was to be the ultimate test of the U.S. Army's new combat doctrine of air mobility. The 1st Cavalry Division was the most mobile force in the history of warfare, with more than 400 helicopters capable of airlifting an entire infantry brigade into combat. While designed primarily as light infantry, the 1st Cavalry could also deliver massive firepower with its artillery, aerial rocket artillery, and helicopter gun ships. The Air Cav also boasted three battalions of paratroopers organized into the 1st Airborne Brigade with the capability of parachuting into combat if necessary.

Profile of the Enemy

The division faced a for-
midable foe in the NVA, who
many considered to be the best
light infantry in the world.
These soldiers from the North
were well-trained, well-
equipped, and well motivated.
They flooded down the Ho
Chi Minh trail into the 1st
Cav's area of operations,
which stretched from the
Cambodian border to the
South China Sea. While they

NVA soldiers prepare for attack on the Special Forces Camp

lacked the firepower and the
mobility of the Cav, they had an intimate knowledge of the terrain, the
benefit of sanctuaries across the Cambodian border, and the ability to
engage in battle only when they saw or created in a tactical advantage.
If they saw an opportunity to defeat an American unit due to advantages in combat strength, terrain superiority, or battlefield surprise,
they would be quick to engage. They were also very patient and would
shadow American units with probes and harassing fire in an effort to
break down morale and combat discipline to create a tactical advantage
they could immediately exploit.

The Proud 1st Cav

Alpha Company, 2nd Battalion (Airborne), 8th Cavalry, was part of
the 1st Cavalry Division's parachute brigade. Alpha Company was
well-trained, well-led, and its ranks were filled with some of the toughest soldiers in South Vietnam, many of whom were veterans of the 11th
Air Assault training at Fort Benning, Georgia. Others came from crack
stateside units, such as the 101st and 82nd Airborne Divisions. A great
majority of the senior noncommissioned officers (NCOs) and officers
were combat veterans. Ranger tabs, Pathfinder patches, and Recondo
brands were common amongst the cadre. The NVA soldiers were good,
but man for man, they were not equal to the troopers of the 1st Air
Cavalry.

The long and proud history of the 1st Cavalry Division places it at the pinnacle of the American military experience. In its air-mobile configuration during the Vietnam War, the division made an enormous contribution, paid for in the blood and sweat of its own, to its proud storied tradition. The 1st Cavalry engaged in combat operations in Vietnam for more than seven years, the longest of any division in American history. It was the first division-sized unit to

Troopers take a break between air assaults

arrive in Vietnam and the last to furl its colors and return stateside. The 1st Cav suffered more than 5,000 killed in action. Almost 10 percent of the names engraved on the Vietnam Memorial are 1st Cav troopers. About 15,000 division soldiers were wounded in action. The 1st Cavalry Division was awarded the Presidential Unit Citation for its heroic and aggressive victories against the NVA during the Pleiku Campaign of November 1965.

This is a story about the men of Alpha Company and their first fateful days of combat. The Alpha Raiders along with their comrades of the 1st Brigade would first encounter the NVA during the battles of Pleiku Province. They were an enemy the 1st Cavalry Division would engage time and time again over the next seven years. As part of the division's 1st Brigade, Alpha Company, 2nd Battalion (Airborne), 8th Cavalry put the air-assault concept to its first critical test in battle. These initial engagements with the NVA would culminate in the epic clashes at Landing Zone (LZ) X-Ray and LZ Albany in mid-November 1965.

NVA Attacks Pleiku

It was just before midnight on October 19, 1965, that the NVA attacked the Plei Me Special Forces Camp in Pleiku Province. Heavy machine gun fire and a mortar barrage announced the attack, which was part of a bold Communist initiative designed to cut South Vietnam in two and gain control of the important Central Highlands. The soldiers from the North flooded across the Cambodian border in three regiments capable of divisional-sized operations. The NVA had not fielded units of this strength since defeating the French at Dien Bien Phu 11 years earlier.

This large NVA formation consisted of the 33rd, 32nd, and 66th Regiments, as well as various administrative and support units. The 33rd Regiment's mission was to attack the Special Forces Camp at Plei Me, while the 32nd was ordered to ambush and destroy any relief column sent to the camp from Pleiku. Although the NVA attack on the Special Forces Camp was bloody and determined, its attempt to completely destroy the camp or capture Pleiku City failed. The NVA ambush of the relief column was also thwarted and suffered greatly from U.S. Air Force F-100 air strikes, accurate Air Cavalry artillery support, as well as Huey gun ships delivering devastating close air support.

Airborne Troopers Deployed

Even though the North Vietnamese goal of capturing control of the Central Highlands had been stymied, the American high command in Saigon was still very concerned that a main force NVA unit was rampaging across Pleiku Province at will. So, at his headquarters in Nha Trang, Major General Stanley "Swede" Larsen, Commander of Task Force Alfa, ordered the commander of the 1st Cavalry Division, Major General Harry W. O. Kinnard, to secure Pleiku City. The initial Air Cav unit that Major General Kinnard deployed to Pleiku was a composite outfit named Task Force Ingram, which was deployed on October 21 by

The Plei Me Special Forces Camp

airlift and had completely secured the major U.S. base at Camp Holloway by October 23. Task Force Ingram consisted of 2/12th Cavalry, commanded by Lieutenant Colonel Earl Ingram, the task force's namesake, Battery B of the 2/17th Artillery, a weapons section of 1/9th Cavalry, and elements of the 8th Engineers.

While this move was underway, Major General Kinnard, sensing that a decisive operation was imminent, made preparations to deploy the division's 1st Airborne Brigade to Pleiku. The brigade had been operating in the Binh Khe area east of the An Khe base camp along

Captain Roger McElroy, A Company CO

Route 19, the major east-west road through the Central Highlands. So, a small detachment of the 1st Airborne Brigade, led by acting Brigade Commander Lieutenant Colonel Harlow Clark, along with the entire 2nd Battalion (Airborne), 8th Cavalry, commanded by Lieutenant Colonel James Nix and two firing batteries of the 2/19th Artillery, were immediately extracted from the Vinh Thanh Valley at 1500 hours on October 23. The unit closed in by air on Camp Holloway at midnight to assume operational control from Task Force Ingram.

The 1st Airborne Brigade's area of operation covered approximate-

Chu Pong Massif, a favorite infiltration route

ly 1,500 square miles of flat rolling terrain. The Ia Drang, Ia Puch, and Ia Kreng rivers, and an extensive network of small streams, all flowed to the west and southwest across the Cambodian border into the Mekong River. The dominating terrain feature of the brigade's operational area was the Chu Pong Massif, which had long been favored by the NVA as an important infiltration and marshalling area. On October 24, the paratroopers of A Company, 2nd Battalion (Airborne), 8th Cavalry, under the command of Captain Roger McElroy, boarded choppers and air assaulted to a firebase along Highway 14, where they provided security for an artillery battery of the 2/19th. The mission of the artillery was to provide support for the South Vietnamese relief column advancing toward the Plei Me Special Forces Camp from Pleiku City.

Securing Chu Ho

After spending two days providing security for the big guns of the 2/19th, the troopers of A Company were air assaulted to a large open field located between the Special Forces Camp and Plei Me village, where they encountered an appalling stench of dead bodies upon exiting their choppers. Dead NVA soldiers were everywhere, many of whom were burned beyond recognition as a result of napalm air strikes and white phosphorus artillery rounds. The troopers had no sooner landed when

Specialist Juan Fernandez

they were ordered to join B Company for an assault on a position designated Objective Cherry on nearby Chu Ho Mountain. The assault up the mountain took about an hour, and the troopers attacked under supporting mortar fire. As they advanced, the soldiers of Alpha Company passed many dead North Vietnamese killed over the previous week's fighting. Unfortunately, the assault resulted in the 2nd Battalion's first combat casualty, Staff Sergeant Charles Rose of B Company, who was killed on October 27, 1965, by a sniper while leading his squad in an assault against an enemy position.

After securing Chu Ho, the troopers of A Company maintained their position on the mountain for the next several days and experienced only occasional mortar and sniper fire from the enemy. On the morning of October 31, the company troopers were moved to LZ Paris, where they conducted aggressive patrols in search of the elusive enemy. That afternoon, a lone enemy soldier approached the A Company perimeter with hands raised in surrender. The soldier was taken into custody and fed some rations, as he awaited the arrival of Battalion Commander Lieutenant Colonel Nix, for interrogation. The colonel's command chopper landed, and as Nix stepped from his helicopter, the NVA prisoner jumped to his feet, clicked his heels, and snapped a perfect salute. The Colonel seemed impressed and returned the salute.

"As I watched that scene," recalls Specialist Juan Fernandez, a rifleman with the 3rd Platoon, "A sergeant standing next to me whistled and remarked, "Hot damn, that ain't a farmer, that's hardcore NVA infantry!"

The next day, a platoon of the 1/9th Cav overran a regimental aid station 6 miles southwest of Plei Me, killing 15 enemy soldiers and capturing another 15. This rifle platoon had air assaulted into the area in response to the sightings of small groups of NVA by 9th Cav scout helicopters. The fighting was at close quarters, too close for rocket, artillery, or tactical air support. Reinforcements were committed, and platoons from 1/12th (recently returned from Operation Shiny Bayonet), 2/12th (veterans of Operation Gibralter in September), and 2/8th Cav landed late in the afternoon, followed by two additional platoons from 2/12th Cav. This contact resulted in 99 enemy killed and an additional 183 estimated wounded.

Captain Ted Danielsen led night air assault into LZ Mary

Drawing First Blood Again

On the night of November 3, the 1/9th Cav was once again able to pick a fight and draw first blood. At approximately 2100 hours, 9th Cav troopers pulled off a perfectly executed ambush against a full company of NVA infantrymen, who were caught in a wall of lead. The 9th Cavalry ambush patrol swiftly returned to its base at LZ Mary and went to work to strengthen its perimeter.

At 2230 hours, LZ Mary came under heavy attack by three companies of NVA regulars. By midnight, the perimeter was in grave danger of being overrun. So, the Alphagators of A Company, 1st Battalion (Airborne), 8th Cavalry, commanded by West Pointer Captain Ted Danielsen, were tasked with rescuing the besieged troopers of the scrappy 9th Cav. Captain Danielsen's mission was not only heroic, but it was also historic, as he led his men in the first night combat air assault in the history of helicopter warfare. After several hours of fierce close combat, the enemy melted back into the jungle having failed in the attempt to overwhelm the Air Cav troopers. An estimated 250 NVA soldiers were killed as a result of the ambush and subsequent fight at LZ Mary, with an equal number of enemy wounded, while the combined casualties of the 1/8th and 9th Cavalry were fewer than a dozen.

Airborne Warriors Taste Combat

In early November 1965, Alpha Company, 2nd Battalion (Airborne), 8th Cavalry, was conducting air assault operations searching for enemy forces in the vicinity of the Plei Me Special Forces Camp. The 2nd Battalion headquarters along with A Battery, 2/19th Field Artillery were located at LZ Cavalair. Elements of the Alpha Raiders were widely dispersed in the vicinity of that landing zone. On the morning of November 4, the company was airlifted to LZ Cavalair in order to provide security for the battalion headquarters and the artillery battery.

Later that morning, Delta Company's reconnaissance platoon engaged a significant enemy force in a fierce firefight about 800 meters

LT Holtslag registers artillery around Plei Me Special Forces Camp

north of Cavalair. As the firefight intensified, the executive
officer of Delta Company,
Lieutenant Frank Trapnell, led
a relief force to support the
platoon. The 2nd Platoon of A
Company, which was part of
this force, swept into the
North Vietnamese base camp
that had been the source of the
intense fire into the American
force, and engaged in a close-
range firefight with a large
NVA unit. Realizing that the

Alpha Company Assault

Trapnell relief force and the recon platoon were fully committed against
a superior enemy force, the 2/8th Commander Lieutenant Colonel Nix,
ordered the rest of A Company to join in the attack from the southeast.
Alpha Company Commander Captain Roger McElroy led the 1st and
3rd Platoons in a rapid sweep toward the sounds of the ongoing battle.

The day was hot without a cloud in the sky. The troopers of A
Company dropped their rucksacks on the LZ and carried only weapons,
ammunition, and canteens into the fight. The terrain, dotted with tall trees
interspersed with waist-high grass, was unlike the triple canopy jungle
that characterized most of the 1st Cav area of operations. Visibility ranged
from 50 to 100 meters. The terrain's contour, which was quite rocky,

included a series of small hills and gullies. But neither the trees, the foliage, nor
the terrain were deterrents to ground
movement. Captain McElroy put out
some flank guards, and the column
moved so fast that many of the troopers
were becoming winded from the heat
and the rapid pace.

Point man Specialist Leonard
Lawrence, who led the A Company
advance, was followed close behind by
Specialist Juan Fernandez, Private First
Class Hector Colon, Sergeant Walter
Hester, and the remainder of the 3rd
Platoon. As Specialist Lawrence crossed

Pointman Leonard Lawrence a ridgeline, he noticed 30 or 40 bushes to his left front that seemed to be moving. Sergeant Hester called for Specialist Lawrence to halt and to watch the trees. Sergeant Hester then fired a single shot from the M14 sniper rifle he was carrying. A North Vietnamese soldier fell with a thud from a tree just in front of the A Company formation. With this shot, Sergeant Hester scored the Alpha Raiders' first kill of an enemy soldier in Vietnam.

At that point, the wooded area beyond the A Company position erupted with the roar of automatic weapons fire, and the Airborne Warriors' first taste of combat was at hand. This initial contact with the enemy began on the blazing hot afternoon of November 4, 1965. Platoon Sergeant Norman Welch led the 3rd Platoon into a dry creek bed, which allowed some protection from the enemy fire that was now coming from all directions. The initial barrage of fire from the NVA formation caused several casualties among the Alpha troopers.

Heroes of the Campaign

Private First Class Joe Brown, a 17-year-old artillery forward observer attached to A Company, felt very proud of himself, as the Airborne Warriors left their landing zone on the march toward the firefight. His team leader, Lieutenant Joe Holtslag, was providing fire support from a chopper overhead of the ground units as requested by Captain McElroy. Holtslag knew that Brown was proficient in adjusting artillery fire and recommended to McElroy that Brown accompany the ground unit in case close in support was needed. McElroy agreed. Brown

*Private First Class
Joe Brown*

recalls, "Having the Lieutenant send me to do his job was more than trust; it was a giant compliment."

As the firefight started, Brown heard a man to his right yelling for a medic. He saw the wounded American lying under a tree to his front. Brown crawled forward and reached the creek bed where the 3rd Platoon had established its defensive position. Several other wounded troopers were scattered in front of the creek. The young artilleryman sprayed the treetops with a magazine of M16 fire and dashed out to pull the wounded cavalryman into the shelter of the creek bed.

A short distance from Brown but in the same creek bed, Platoon

*Sergeant First Class
Norman Welch*

Sergeant Welch had rallied the 3rd Platoon, which began to bring heavy and effective fire on the North Vietnamese. Welch set up one squad as a base of fire in the creek bed, and he, along with his radiotelephone operator, Private First Class Ronald Luke, led two squads in an assault up the ridgeline into the enemy position. The North Vietnamese fire was intense, and the cavalry advance was slow. Both Platoon Sergeant Welch and Private First Class Luke were everywhere during this advance into the wall of fire being laid down by the NVA. They pushed forward heroically and were both awarded Silver Stars for their valor that day. Tragically, Private First Class Luke did not survive the day and received his medal posthumously.

Remembering the Fight

Private First Class Dave Dement, remembers the day vividly. He recalls mentioning to Private First Class Jacob Townsend, with whom he shared a defensive position the previous night, that it was his girlfriend Betsy's 18th birthday. As they both prepared for the battle, PFC Dement's squad leader, Staff Sergeant John Dailey, assigned him to carry two cans of ammunition for one of the platoon's M60 machine guns:

*Private First Class
David Dement*

"I was told to stay with Private First Class Smith, our machine gunner, and Private First Class Fred Moore, the assistant gunner." Dement remembers thinking to himself, "This is just what I need, more weight to carry. I was already carrying 460 rounds of M16 ammo, twice the normal load." The column was moving so fast that Dement often had to run to keep up. "With the heat, my heavy load, and the pace, I was exhausted as we approached the sound of the ongoing battle."

For Dement, the battle started when he saw Staff Sergeant Isaac

Guest's squad, the Guest Gorillas, chasing down several NVA riflemen who had fired the opening volleys. Dement joined the chase and recalls being in disbelief. "This can't be real; it must be a training exercise. When I began to realize this was the real thing, my adrenaline began to rush and my heart was pounding so fast I thought my chest would explode. We ran right into the NVA position. All hell was breaking loose. I think Sergeant Guest saved our lives by pushing so hard and taking us out of the principal killing zone."

The Mighty 3rd Platoon

The ferocity of the firefight intensified as the afternoon wore on. The 3rd Platoon was inflicting a heavy toll on the enemy force. Specialist Lawrence, along with Staff Sergeant Guest, fired magazine after magazine into the dug-in positions to their front. An NVA machine gunner began pounding away at the tree that Specialist Lawrence was using for cover. Private First Class Douglas Smith, who was manning an M60 machine gun, cut down the NVA gunner but not before Specialist Lawrence had been hit with fragments of the tree blown into his arms and chest by the incoming fire.

Sergeant Art Miller carrying AN/PRC-25 radio

Sergeant Art Miller was a fire team leader in the 3rd Platoon. He recalls the North Vietnamese force being arrayed in a horseshoe formation with heavy machine gun fire at each of the rear corners. Sergeant Miller was doing double duty that day, filling in as forward observer for the company's mortar platoon. Carrying an AN/PRC 25 radio on his back made him a prize target for the North Vietnamese gunners. When the formation first came under fire, Sergeant Miller was pinned down, and every time he tried to move, his radio would be the target of incoming fire. After one enemy volley, Platoon Sergeant Welch shouted over to Sergeant Miller asking if he had any smoke grenades. Since Sergeant Miller had one smoke and one white phosphorous grenade, Platoon Sergeant Welch said, "Count to three, pop the grenades, and run like hell for the creek bed!" Sergeant Miller tossed the grenades and ran back toward the creek bed. He was knocked off his feet by enemy rounds hitting his radio, but was able to make it back to the shelter of the creek bed.

While the North Vietnamese fire pinned down Sergeant Miller, Private First Class Dement, and his machine gun crew were located in a small depression, their M60 burning through so many rounds that the barrel of the gun was smoking. Incoming rounds were popping over their heads from almost every direction. Dement took cover behind his two cans of ammo trying to avoid the North Vietnamese gunfire. Sergeant Garland Tankersley ordered Smith and his gun crew to move to higher ground to cover Guest's squad so they could pull back to a safer position. Smith, Moore, and Dement ran for a small knoll, while other 3rd Platoon troopers laid down a base of fire to cover their movement.

Smith and Moore made it to the top of the knoll and set up their machine gun. Dement scrambled up to join his crew but slipped on some rocks and tumbled down the knoll, ammo cans still in his hands. Sergeant Tankersley yelled at the young private to get the damn ammo up to the gun. "I scrambled back up to join Smith and Moore," recalls Dement. "When I reached the top, I saw Smith lying face down, his back covered with blood. Moore was slumped against a tree on his knees. I thought they were both dead."

At that point, Dement felt completely alone. All he could do was run down the knoll once again looking for help. "I saw Sergeant

Artillery "fire for effect" rounds impacting on NVA positions,
November 4, 1965

Tankersley at the bottom of the small hill," Dement continues. "He told me to get the hell back up the knoll and get that gun working. As I crawled back up, I saw our platoon medic working on Smith. I told him they were both dead. He replied that Smith wasn't dead, only wounded. I got to the M60, but its butt plate was shot off and wouldn't fire. I crawled down that godforsaken knoll for the third time. At that point, I realized I hadn't fired a shot. I couldn't believe it."

When Dement reached the bottom of the knoll, he linked up again with Sergeant Tankersley. Heavy sniper fire was coming from the treetops on a ridgeline to their front. Sergeant Tankersley yelled to Dement to start killing the "sons of bitches." Dement emptied magazine after magazine, shooting at anything that moved.

As the Alpha Raiders poured heavy fire into the NVA positions, the incoming fire began to die down. Platoon Sergeant Welch and other 3rd Platoon troopers in exposed positions were told to move back to a nearby creek bed that would offer more protection. Dement was ordered to provide protective fire while the exposed Americans withdrew, but realized he had used all 460 rounds he had carried into the battle. "When I had pulled back from my position to the nearby creek bed, I asked Private First Class Johnny Booze if he had any extra ammo. He reached into his pockets and pulled out handfuls of loose rounds. I needed magazines. Fortunately, this was no problem; they were all over the ground."

Big guns of the Air Cav pound enemy positions

Alpha Raiders Artillery Tragedy

With the enemy fire intensifying once again, Captain McElroy needed some artillery support to suppress the incoming rounds from the North Vietnamese position. Brown, the artillery forward observer, moved along the creek bed to link up with McElroy and the rest of the company command group clustered against the creek wall. McElroy was on the radio and checking map coordinates. Neither he nor Brown were sure of their precise location and couldn't fire any artillery until they had a good location to spot the rounds. Brown crawled up the creek bed to try to get a fix on his location, but the elephant grass was too high to spot any landmarks. He then tried to call his supporting artillery battery, but not only was the range on his radio severely limited, but his antenna had also been shot off. Numerous times he tried to raise Shining Star 43, the call sign for Alpha Battery, 2/19th Artillery, but heard no reply. Finally, a faint voice on the radio responded, "This is Shining Star 43; we have your fire mission; go ahead." Brown asked them to fire a concentration at the location that Lieutenant Holtslag had registered a short while before, which he knew was well to his front. At this point, the Alpha Raiders were minutes away from a tragedy that would haunt them, even 40 years later.

The first artillery rounds landed several hundred meters to Brown's north. He then directed Shining Star 43 to drop 100 meters and go left 50 meters. The artillery fire was beginning to pound into the

*Air Cav Artillery has a devastating effect on the landscape
as well as the enemy*

North Vietnamese positions. Brown then ordered another adjustment even closer to his position and a "fire-for-effect" barrage with the entire battery letting loose on the hapless enemy. Several more adjustments and fires for effect were having a devastating impact. Brown ordered one more volley, and then something went terribly wrong. One of the incoming rounds smashed right into the north edge of the creek bed, and deadly shrapnel and debris ripped through the 3rd Platoon position. The ground felt like it was falling out from under the creek bed, and wounded cavalrymen were everywhere. Several were dead, including Private First Class Ronald Luke, Private First Class Alan Barnett, Private First Class Carl Daniels, and Specialist Dennis Long. Brown felt nauseous at the destruction this errant round had inflicted, as he saw several troopers helping mortally wounded team leader Sergeant James Jasinski, whose head was a mass of blood. A number of survivors comforted Brown, for whatever had caused this tragedy, it was certainly not the fault of this valiant artilleryman whose initiative and courage enabled the Airborne Warriors of Alpha Company to defeat a vastly superior enemy force. The impact of this ferocious artillery attack broke the back of the enemy position and forced the enemy to withdraw with heavy casualties.

Dave Dement was a short distance down the creek bed from where the short round hit. He was dazed and covered in dirt and debris, at first unable to see due to the dense dust kicked up by the exploding artillery shell. "I finally regained my composure and knew I needed to

Joe Holtslag displays a captured AK-47

Artillery Forward Observer Joe Holtslag

help the wounded guys," he recalls. "Bodies were everywhere. I looked down and saw the body of our Vietnamese interpreter with his leg almost detached. When I picked up the body, the leg fell off, so I dropped the body and stepped back. The images were horrifying."

Lieutenant Holtslag remembered landing in the vicinity of A Company troopers to help evacuate their wounded: "I met them on their way back from the forward edge of the battle area. They were carrying their dead and wounded, bloodied and bedraggled, but certainly not defeated."

Letters Home

The Airborne Warriors of Alpha Company had met the enemy for the first time. They had been tested and not found wanting. The next day, Lieutenant Holtslag wrote this letter home to his wife and children:

"Hi Sandy, Tracy, and Jay,

This is going to be short. Just a few lines to tell you about a hero I know. My Radio Telephone Operator (RTO) Joe Brown, will be nominated for a medal by Captain McElroy.

We were on a search and destroy mission yesterday. I was giving the company artillery support from a helicopter overhead. I had been up for about 2 hours and firing various artillery missions. As a result, I think there were 30 killed by the artillery. I had sent Joe Brown with the company on foot. The company was caught in an ambush just as I had to return for fuel. I told Joe Brown he was on his own and to give the company artillery support. I had heard there were about 20 enemy snipers in trees and they had completely encircled our company. Our men were being picked off like flies when Brown called in a fire mission, adjusted the rounds in (almost on top of) them, and killed quite a few of the enemy soldiers. The rest of them took off. I monitored the whole thing on the radio while refueling. Hon, I was never as proud of anyone in my life as I was of Brown. He really kept his head, did everything he was taught, and saved the lives of many of our soldiers.

As fate would have it, it didn't turn out to be a bed of roses. As I said, the rounds were real close, and one of them came into a ravine right behind Brown and Captain McElroy, plus the rest of the head-quarters element where they were pinned down and had the wounded. The round killed three of our wounded instantly and wounded four more. Brown saw this happen and went temporarily into shock. He thought it was his fault and that he had killed his buddies. When I got on the ground, they were sending Charlie Company in to help evacu-ate the wounded. When I got to Brown, he was quite emotionally upset. I can only imagine how he felt. He was sick and throwing up. We got him out with the rest of the company, and I sat him down and had a long talk with him. Major Anthony (Artillery Battalion XO) came out to investigate what had happened and also spoke to Brown. We finally convinced him that what he had done was to save the lives of every man in that company. I'm real proud to say that I trained him and he's a fine man for 17 (he'll be 18 tomorrow). I had him evacuated this morn-ing to have him checked by a doctor. He was running a fever and had a terrible headache. The medic thinks it is emotional and physical exhaustion. He said he'd be back in a couple of days. The Major con-gratulated me on the fine job Brown did and the company commander

Joe Brown inspects the lower torso of an NVA
in what was left of his foxhole.

is a believer of artillery support at this time. He said, and I quote 'If it hadn't been for the artillery, we would all be dead now.' As it was we ended up with 9 dead and 16 wounded.

Honey, that was the first time I wasn't with the company commander. God must be watching over me. I'm grateful that I didn't have to experience what these men did. It was a terrifying two hours for them. Those NVA soldiers and their ambushes sure can do it to you. We are really coming out on top, though. The VC and

Joe Holtslag with Vietnamese interpreter

NVA are walking into our camps and surrendering right and left. I think we are on the road to victory. I hope so.

By the way, Brown risked his life getting into position to observe the rounds coming in on the enemy; fortunately, he did. He moved from the exact spot where the short round hit and did all the damage. As I said, Brown is quite a man.

That's it for now, hon. Kiss the kids and give them my love.

I'll always love you,

Joe"

The same day, 19-year-old rifleman Specialist Leonard Lawrence from Cinco, West Virginia, wrote home to his mother, recounting the previous day's battle:

"Fri. 5 Nov.

My Darling Mother,

I thought I should write you a letter to let you know I'm o.k. Since we were in a little battle on the 4th from about 12 o'clock till about 6 p.m.

This would be midnight till 6 a.m., and I felt you were praying for me all of the time. Mom, don't worry about me if I don't make it because in the heat of this battle when I was pinned down for about 2 hrs., God and me had a nice long talk, and He and I have everything straight between us.

In our battle, we had 5 killed and 12 wounded out of 34 men in my platoon, and the only thing that happened to me was I got a piece of bark off the tree I was behind, in my finger that a bullet knocked loose.

Well, Mom, it's almost dark, and I'm going to have to sign off for now. Answer soon, and I'll write when I get a chance. I'll see you in 8 months.

Until then it's,
LOVE
LEONARD

P.S.
I love you"

Mission Accomplished

On November 9, after two full weeks of continuous enemy contact, the paratroopers of the 1st Brigade had accomplished their mission of securing Pleiku City, and operational responsibility for the area was assigned to the 3rd Brigade. During this transition, the enemy regiments were reorganizing after their defeat at Plei Me, the failed ambush of the relief column, and the subsequent defeat inflicted on them by the paratroopers of the 1st Airborne Brigade.

On November 11, the enemy took stock and found that the 32nd Regiment was still a cohesive fighting force despite casualties sustained during the attempted ambush of the ARVN relief column that was moving to reinforce the Plei Me Special Forces Camp. The 33rd Regiment lost 890 men out of its original 2,200, with 100 missing, 13 of its 18 anti-aircraft machine guns, and 5 out of 9 82mm mortars. Its shattered ranks required reorganization to form an effective fighting force. The 66th Regiment only lost 98 men during the battle of November 3-4, and, as a result, provided the major remaining cutting

*The NVA were defeated,
yet defiant*

edge of the NVA force. The 32nd was located north of the Ia Drang, the 33rd maintained its positions just north of the Chu Pong, and the battalions of the 66th were strung along the northern bank of the Ia Drang. The stage was now set for the bloodiest battles of the Vietnam War.

III
Don's Homecoming

7th Cavalry troopers fight their way into LZ X-ray

On the morning of November 14, 1965, the 1st Battalion of the 7th Cavalry air assaulted into the Valley of the Ia Drang to the cheers of "Garry Owen." Over the next four days, the troopers of the 1st and 2nd Battalion of the 7th Cavalry, along with their brothers of the 5th Cavalry, fought at LZs X-ray and Albany, America's largest battles since the Korean War. The men of the 3rd Brigade stood shoulder to shoulder, fought, and defeated a vastly superior enemy force that was fanatically committed to the complete annihilation of the cavalry battalions they engaged. The number of American casualties at X-ray and Albany was great but far fewer than the number of heroes born of those terrible battles.

The Heroes of Pleiku

The Pleiku Campaign eventually involved the entire division and ended with the First Sergeants of 15 battalion, batteries, and squadrons crossing names off their company morning reports. The troopers who lived through the Pleiku Campaign returned to Camp Radcliff at An Khe. The wounded were sent to hospitals in Vietnam, Japan, and Hawaii, while the severely wounded were sent to stateside military hospitals. Halfway around the world from Vietnam, hundreds of American families were being notified that their soldiers were returning. Those who died in the Pleiku Campaign were being sent home to their loved ones.

A Returning Soldier's Story

"Donald Cornett was my brother," recalls his sister Carole. "He was my older brother, and, in every sense of the word, he was my big brother. It was a responsibility he took seriously and a job he did well. Don was a person I could always count on. We grew up as military brats, and all the traveling around never gave us the chance to make lasting friendships. Out of necessity we became our own best friends. Don was a person everyone looked up to. In school he was a natural leader and a good student. He was tall, athletic, and handsome. Don excelled at everything he tried. It wasn't that things came easily to Don; he simply tried harder than most. We both attended McNeese State College in Lake Charles, Louisiana.

Soldiers returning home to their families

Carole and Don Cornett,
ages 6 and 8, respectively

Don was two years ahead of me and was considered a big man on campus. His senior year he was elected president of the student body. His major was history, but his passion was ROTC. He was a born soldier, and, in his senior year, he became the ROTC Colonel of the Pershing Rifles Drill Team, an honor of which he was very proud.

Upon graduation from McNeese, Don was commissioned as a second lieutenant in the U.S. Army, and, because of his ROTC accomplishments, he received a coveted Regular Army commission. He was now a soldier, and he approached it with the energy and enthusiasm of a zealot. He volunteered for Ranger school, and, upon graduation, Don was assigned to the 2nd Battalion, 9th Infantry of the 2nd Infantry Division, stationed at Fort Benning, Georgia. He was a brand new Airborne Ranger second lieutenant, and could hardly wait to begin the challenge of becoming the best soldier possible. Like most infantry second lieutenants, his first assignment was as a platoon leader, a job he really loved.

Earlier the year before, Don had married his college sweetheart, Sylvia, and they were expecting their first child later that fall. Don wrote often, telling me how hard his unit was training. They were involved in a new concept called 'Airmobile' and were training with a unit called the 11th Air Assault. They spent a lot of time in or around helicopters, and Don mentioned he was considering going to Army flight school. Don loved to fly. He had taken flight lessons as part of his ROTC training and had received a civilian pilot's license his senior year in college.

'This helicopter thing was the wave of the future,' Don wrote in one letter to me.

It all sounded so exciting, and I was pleased Don was doing some-

Don on the McNeese State
Varsity football team in 1962

Don and Sylvia at Ft. Benning shortly after their wedding

thing he truly enjoyed.

In the spring of 1965, exciting things were happening in my life as well. I was preparing to graduate with my B.S. in Nursing from McNeese State and start my first real job at Charity Hospital right here in Lake Charles. It was later that spring when Don wrote that his unit of the 2nd Infantry Division was being redesignated as the 2nd Battalion of the 7th Cavalry of the 1st Cavalry Division Airmobile. The 7th Cavalry, Don wrote, was Custer's old outfit, but told me that I shouldn't worry because it had earned a distinguished combat record in both World War II and Korea. He also added the Air Cav was on alert for deployment to Vietnam that summer.

My father called from North Carolina; he had talked to Don at Fort Benning, and they had set a date for a family reunion in Georgia. This would be the first time we had gathered as a family since college. Dad gave me the directions to Don's and the date. He, Mom, and my younger sister, Peggy, would be driving south. I was looking forward to the reunion with enthusiasm.

Don, Sylvia, and their infant son Kevin, lived at the Camellia Apartments, outside of Fort Benning. The apartment complex was full of young Air Cavalry officers and their families. All of them, it seemed, were also on their way to Vietnam. It was a special time. There were lots of parties and cookouts with Don's friends and their families. There was a lot of positive energy, and all of Don's buddies were enthusiastic about the upcoming deployment. They all had great confidence in their training and were eager to show the enemy what the Air Cav could do.

Don as McNeese State University's student body president

That evening before we left for home, Dad and Don sat together talking about Vietnam. My father had retired from the Army as a lieutenant colonel several years earlier. Dad was not an emotional man, but in his talk with Don, I sensed real fear and apprehension. Don sensed it also and tried to reassure my Dad that any conflict would be short lived once the enemy encountered the Air Cavalry. I remember how Dad told him the importance of not only relying on his sergeants but also listening to them. Don agreed with him and told him that most of his senior NCOs were World War II and Korean War combat vets. The next morning we said our goodbyes to

Platoon leader Don Cornett aboard transport USNS **Maurice Rose**

Don, Sylvia, and Kevin. I remember how proud we all felt of Don and how I was looking forward to our next reunion upon his return home from overseas.

August 1965, Don and his battalion boarded the USNS *Maurice Rose*, for their month-long ocean voyage to Vietnam. I didn't hear from Don again for about six weeks. It was mid-September when a letter arrived telling me about life aboard ship. He wrote that he and his unit were setting up a huge base camp in a place called An Khe. He described a giant

ROTC cadet aviators: Don is in the back row, far right

airfield that was being built that everyone called the 'Golf Course.' It was going to be the largest helicopter base in the world. He also explained that he and his unit were doing a lot of training in and around a place called 'Happy Valley' [the Vinh Thanh Valley] and that it was good to be back on dry land again after having spent a month aboard ship. He closed by asking me to say 'Hi' to everyone in Lake Charles and promised to write again soon. It was a wonderful letter. I read it over and over and even carried it in my purse so others could also read it. It was as if somehow that letter was proof that everything was going to be all right.

Don on patrol in   A couple of weeks later I received another
"Happy Valley," Vietnam letter from Don with a couple of photographs.
One was of him in combat gear and another was of a scorpion he found in his bedroll. He wrote that things were fine, and he promised to write again soon.

It was about a week or so later when I was getting ready for my shift at the hospital that the radio caught my attention. The network news was reporting a major battle, taking place in Vietnam. I heard the words '1st Air Cavalry' and '7th Cavalry,' and my blood froze. I immediately called my parents in North Carolina. My father answered the telephone and I blurted out, 'Have you heard the news? Don's unit is in combat! It was on the radio!'

The McNeese State University ROTC color guard escorts Don's body

'Now relax,' my father said. 'It was on the TV news last night, and your mother was in such a state that I called an old Army friend at Fort Benning, and the unit involved was the 1st Battalion of the 7th Cavalry; Don's in the 2nd Battalion of the 7th.'

For the next several days I would go to work, listening for the news before and after my shift. My parents called me almost every day, or I called them. My mom called one Thursday morning and told me she knew Don was dead; she just knew it. Dad dismissed it, but I certainly worried more. No one can deny that there's a special connection between mothers and sons, and, of course, Don being her first born, had a special bond with Mom. About a week after the battles of LZ X-ray and LZ Albany, our family received our official notification. My father called me sobbing. He had just gotten off the phone with Don's wife, Sylvia, in Houston. She had just been delivered a telegram. The delivery man had no idea what he was delivering until, as he was leaving, he heard Sylvia scream. She was alone in her apartment with her baby son, Kevin, when she read that Don had been killed. Her parents lived about 60 miles away, and my parents were in North Carolina. It was a terrible time for her to be alone and separated from family. I didn't leave my apartment for several days. I was numb with grief.

My parents drove from North Carolina to Sylvia's in Houston, where they arranged for Don's memorial service at McNeese State. It was to be held in the same church that Don and Sylvia were married in only a couple of years before. There were many problems in arranging for Don's return. We could not get an exact date for his arrival. We were told there were not enough officers to escort all the bodies coming home for burial. The protocol is for a soldier of equal or higher rank to escort the remains.

Finally, we got a date, all the arrangements were completed, and we were notified that Don would arrive by train the next day. We all went to the station in a state of shock, grief, anger, and numb from days of sobbing. When the train arrived, the entire family, along with an ROTC honor guard from the college, stood waiting for the escort officer from the passenger car. I looked down to the end of that awful train and saw a wooden crate containing Don's coffin being unloaded on to a large baggage cart. An officer jumped down from the freight car, unaware of our presence, and placed a flag over the crate. My brother, my soul mate, and the man I admired most in my life, my heart----brought home in a wooden crate. My wonderful brother was coming home in a crate.

The memorial service was held the next day. The church was full to overflowing. People were lined up outside and down the sidewalk into the street. The McNeese ROTC Pershing Rifles provided the honor guard and pallbearers. The local TV station filmed the service, and it was on the local news at 6 and 11 that evening. Don was the first McNeese alumni to die in Vietnam and was still well-remembered in Lake Charles.

The next morning we were up at dawn and put Don back on that awful train for his trip to Arlington National Cemetery. Dad and Mom drove to Arlington with my sister, Peggy. I wanted to be alone, so I followed in my car. We made the occasional stops to eat and sleep. We did not talk to each other except when necessary. We traveled to Arlington in silence, unable to express our grief in words.

Arlington is such a beautiful place. In the summer it's very green and has a certain splendor with its well-manicured grass and its orderly plots containing neat rows of tombstones, each identifying someone whose sacrifice has earned the respect of our country. Arlington seems to change with the seasons. In the spring, it's alive with blossoms, fragrant smells, and cool breezes. In the fall, it becomes somber and stately, almost like a cathedral.

We buried Don on a gray overcast December morning, less than a month from his death in Vietnam. Arlington was a cold bleak place that day. The bitter weather well-matched our moods. The dark sky somehow seemed to capture our desperate grief. The burial was performed with crisp military precision, and when it ended, we walked away from section 35, grave 195, with Sylvia clutching her American Flag, and all of us clinging to each other in our sorrow."

Don buried at Arlington National Cemetery, section 35, grave 195

IV
Base Camp and Beyond

An Khe Village, located 300 hundred miles north of Saigon

In mid-November 1965, Alpha Company returned to the 1st Cav base camp following the Pleiku Campaign. Everyone was amazed at the changes that had taken place at Camp Radcliff during the company's 30-day absence. Gone were the small two-man pup tents that the troopers had slept in upon their arrival in September; in their place stood big platoon-sized tents with wooden floors and cots. The engineers had constructed a beer hall, conveniently located across the dirt road from the entrance to the A Company compound, along with outhouse-type latrines, with shower points for each company. There was even a mess hall in the A Company compound with sit-down seating.

The Greenline

The returning A Company troopers also found tremendous changes along the Greenline, which had been cleared to about a quarter of a mile out from the base camp perimeter into a barren zone called "no man's land."

The hundreds of foxholes the troopers had dug a couple of months earlier as part of the defensive perimeter had all been replaced with bunkers and

*Bill Garlinger at the entrance to
A Company Street*

fortified fighting positions, each with interlocking fields of fire. Every position had preplotted targets for artillery and mortar fire. There was also the ability to call in Huey gun ships that could deliver supporting machine gun and rocket fire to any spot along the Greenline in a moment's notice. As troopers looked out into no man's land, they could see row upon row of razor wire strung with trip flares, with hundreds of claymore mines cemented into position about every 10 meters. The Greenline had evolved into a for-

*The Greenline was a quarter of a mile wide and
ran 17 miles around Camp Radcliff*

Patrolling the "Greenline"

midable defensive barrier that would certainly wreak havoc on any enemy force foolish enough to attack it.

The Greenline was a high maintenance affair and soldiers spent a good portion of their time in base camp on some sort of Greenline duty. Countless nights were spent on Greenline guard, manning one of the many fighting positions assigned to the battalion. Days were spent on Greenline patrols and a couple of times in December, operations were mounted that would push troopers deep into the bush for three to five days.

"On one such mission," recalls Sergeant Art Miller, "we had been out for a couple of days and had patrolled about 15 kilometers from base camp. The afternoon of the second day we were moving in platoon formation leading the rest of the company across an open area that had a large mound in the center of it.

A squad moved around one side of the mound as another squad moved around the opposite side. All of a sudden everyone in both squads was chatting excitedly. I halted my fire team and walked forward cautiously. There, to my surprise, was a real live North Vietnamese Army machine gun team surrounded by smiling Alpha Raiders. Apparently the North Vietnamese had taken a meal break, and, like good soldiers, they had completely dismantled their Russian RPD light machine gun for clean-

Captured enemy machine-gun team

ing. They were completely surprised by our patrol, the gun's many parts laying in perfect order on oilcloth spread on the ground. They obligingly assembled the gun for us and were soon evacuated back to base camp as POWs. I was always glad we had caught them with that gun disassembled; they could have caused some serious damage if the RPD had been operational."

The Crash

"I remember my first Greenline duty," recalls 3rd Platoon trooper Specialist Juan Fernandez. "A couple of squads from my platoon were assigned duty on the Greenline. We were guarding Vietnamese civilian workers as they cleared brush to extend the fields of fire into no

The Huey crashed and burned, killing the crew

man's land. It was good duty. We just lounged around watching the villagers clear brush, trying to keep cool and eating c-rations. Somebody had a cartridge tape machine and we were listening to Diana Ross and the Supremes. Everything was fine; then, all of a sudden, we heard a helicopter approaching.

We looked up to see a Huey coming in at about 50 feet above us with flames and smoke pouring from both sides of its fuselage. Everyone started running for their lives as it came straight toward us. It crashed about 100 feet from me with a huge explosion. Black smoke and flames shot into the air, followed by exploding 2.75" rockets and machine gun ammunition. As I and some of the civilians lay there on the ground, we could see several of the crew struggling to escape the crash, but a tremendous explosion erupted, creating a billowing sheet of flame and smoke, trapping all inside the burning chopper. There were no survivors. I lay flat against the ground listening to the unexploded ordnance cook off. It must have been a half hour before the explosions subsided, and it was safe to approach the crash site. We moved the civilians out of the area and established a perimeter around the crashed Huey. We spent the night guarding the smoldering chopper, and, at dawn, we helped the medics with the grim task of extracting the remains of the dead crew from the charred and twisted wreckage. It was a harsh reminder that you could get killed at base camp as well as in the bush."

Mang Yang Pass

The Mang Yang Pass was where Highway 19 passed along a series of dangerous steep slopes. It threaded itself like a long snake across the 30-foot-wide pass, and it was a location of much importance, inasmuch as whoever controlled the slopes controlled the only road to Pleiku.

The Cav was determined to control Highway 19 and the pass with extensive patrolling of the slopes, manning positions up and down Highway 19 in order to protect this valuable convoy route. Landing zone fire bases were created that could be reinforced quickly by chopper if needed. Missions to the pass could last anywhere from three to five days. Trips to the pass were never fun.

"I remember my first trip to the Mang Yang Pass like it happened last week," recalls Dave Dement. "The entire company was airlifted from An Khe to an LZ on the side of a steep sloping hill along Highway 19. I remember looking down at the road as we flew over and thinking, 'This can't be a highway; it's only about three meters wide.' It looked more like somebody's long, winding driveway back home in North Carolina. The chopper landed us on

The deadly slopes of the Mang Yang Pass

a grassy slope. As the squad exited the chopper, we were ordered to move up the hill just inside the tree line and set up a defensive perimeter.

It was about five minutes after we were in position that I noticed a little brown worm. This was the first time I had seen a worm with suckers on both ends. This little critter was about 3/16" in diameter and 1" long and to many would become one of the most detested life forms in Vietnam. This tiny little creature could bring the toughest, most hardened paratrooper to tears. It was the Vietnam land leech, a slimy, repulsive thing that could somehow attach itself onto the most unlikely parts of your body without any warning. Leeches don't hurt you as they slowly suck your blood, so in most cases you don't feel them---you have to look for them. Once you find them, the excitement starts. My squad had been in position for about a half hour when the 1st squad returned from a recon patrol down the other side of the mountain. As soon as the squad was in position. a couple of the soldiers started hollering as they began stripping off their gear.

I remember Private First Class Johnny Booze running over to me screaming 'Get these damn things off me!' He was covered with leeches. The best way to remove a leech was by putting on salt, mosquito repellent, or burning it with a cigarette. It must have taken me an hour to render Booze leech-free. It was obviously

Highway 19 snaked through the Mang Yang Pass

Johnny's first experience with leeches.

That afternoon the clouds began to move in, blocking out the sun, dropping the temperature rapidly. By evening, cold, fine mist turned into a heavy downpour. I had on my poncho but was soaked to my bones. Whoever designed the poncho apparently never intended to wear it in the rain. The rain runs down inside the poncho, completely soaking you. Under your poncho the damp will start to condensate, and your whole body sort of steams. As night fell, the wind blew harder, and the temperature fell. I thought it didn't get cold in the tropics. None of us were prepared for the winter weather in the Central Highlands of Vietnam.

Around dusk we received orders to move about two clicks down Highway 19; by the time we reached our new position, it was pitch dark. We set up a defensive position. Our portion of the perimeter must have been very long because we had to spread out about 10 meters apart in one-man positions. I was now not only very cold and wet, but also very alone, squatting in the rain by myself in the dark. No one seemed concerned about the NVA being out that night, and I guess our NCOs thought it was too dark for the NVA to see us. The NVA would have to step on us in order to find us. Most likely, the NVA was trying to keep dry and warm as well. I was sitting on my helmet trying to keep my butt out of the cold rain water coming down the hillside.

Truck convoys were a common sight along Highway 19

Sergeant Carerra Christmas Day, Mang Yang Pass

I started to adjust my helmet under my butt in order to be more comfortable and lost my balance, falling off my steel pot into a small hole in the ground. It was so dark that I couldn't make out what it looked like. I felt around in the depression and figured it was about 1" deep, 1 meter wide, and about 1-½ meters long. You would have thought that the hollow would have been full of water, but it wasn't. The slope of the hillside was so steep that the rain was draining out of the small cavity on the lower end as fast as it was coming in. It was very obvious that this depression was blocking the wind from hitting me, so it didn't feel quite as cold as I crouched down in the hole. About midnight I was so cold I began to shiver. My teeth were chattering together so hard that I thought they were going to break; I had never been that cold.

NVA sappers blow up bridge south of the Mang Yang Pass

Sometime after midnight I was about to starve. I had not eaten anything since about 1300 hours the previous day. I was burning a lot of body fuel by shaking so hard. I remembered I had only one can of c-rations--- ham and lima beans. It was a can of the worst tasting crap that anyone could make. There's an old saying, 'hungry enough to eat a raw horse.' I was that hungry. I pulled that can of ham and lima beans out of my chow-sock. I knew from past experience that I needed to open the can on the end that had the grease floating on it. I finished opening the can

Art Miller and his GI Christmas tree

and removed the top and put my fingers in it so that I could feel the grease. Amazingly, I had chosen the correct end. I leaned the can over to one side and skimmed the grease off the top. It's hard to describe the taste of a cold can of ham and limas. I would say it's a combination of Styro- foam and cardboard cooked in too much grease

Private First Class Wilson and Private First Class Singleton chowing down at the new mess hall

Lieutenants Taylor, Holtslag, and Marr
sipping a cold one in "Officers Country."

and seasoned with way too much salt. When you're really hungry, the taste isn't that important. That night those cold ham and lima beans were as good as any steak that I had ever tasted.

That night I did manage to get a few winks in. At first light everyone was up and moving around in order to get their metabolisms working. The rain had tapered off during the night, but it was still as cold as a witch's tail. The wind was still blowing, which made it seem colder. Everyone was talking about the miserable night they had. Someone remarked that the Army had told him it didn't get cold in Vietnam. Someone else said he'd been told that also. We all laughed and someone said, 'I wonder what else they forgot to tell us.'

We were all standing around trying to keep warm and shooting the bull, when I told the story about spending the night in a depression in the ground to keep from freezing.

Some genius spoke up and asked, 'Are you talking about those depressions over there?' as he pointed to what looked like hundreds of them.

I answered, 'Yes.'

He said, 'Didn't you get the word?'

I responded back with, 'What word?'

He said, 'All those depressions are the graves of French soldiers buried in cylinders. You've been sleeping with a dead Frenchman.'

I jokingly commented, 'That's why it was so much warmer in the depression---I was sharing body heat with a corpse!'

As the story goes, during the summer of 1954, a French military detachment, known as Group Mobile 100, was overrun by the 803rd People's Regiment of the NVA, then commonly called the Viet Minh. The French soldiers were all killed and buried in cement cylinders where they fell.

I suddenly became aware of the hundreds of small depressions scattered all along the steep slopes of the pass. The French obviously suffered a tremendous defeat; the graves were everywhere. Later that morning we were told to saddle up and prepare to be picked up by choppers for a return flight to base camp. At about 1100 hours we boarded choppers somewhere along the slopes of the Mang Yang Pass and flew back to Camp Radcliff for hot showers and a turkey dinner with all the fixings. Somebody mentioned it was Thanksgiving Day. It had slipped my mind. Suddenly I was glad that I didn't fill up on ham and limas."

The Jump

After the Cav returned to Camp Radcliff from the Pleiku Campaign, brigade headquarters determined we needed to maintain our jump proficiency and scheduled a parachute jump for the entire 1st Brigade. As Lieutenant Marty Stango recalls, "We were all assembled by company, and then organized into jump sticks of six men each. We chuted up, climbed aboard UH-1D Hueys, and soon the entire sky was filled with parachuting Sky Troopers. This was a definite first for the villagers of An Khe, and they turned out in droves to watch the show.

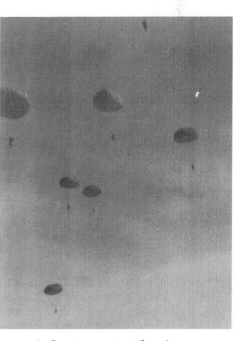

A Company payday jump

The novelty of men loading in choppers, flying into the air, and then jumping out of them quickly created a sort of carnival atmosphere for the villagers. There were some entrepreneurs in the crowd who stood on the ground looking skyward to the descending paratroopers offering to sell them cold Coke and Pepsi from big straw bags filled with ice."

The villagers had a great time and the troopers were all glad for the chance to jump again.

Boom Boom Girls and Ba Muoi Ba Beer

The sleepy little farming village of An Khe had been transformed by the arrival of the 1st Air Cavalry Division. Dozens and dozens of shops and stalls blossomed up and down its muddy streets selling the Air Cav troopers everything under the sun. Jungle fatigues and jungle boots that weren't available through the normal military supply chain could be found in the many thriving black-market shops. Restaurants were plentiful in the village, all selling what they called "hamburgers," but troopers suspected that they were really made from water buffalo. Seamstresses at sewing shops would sew rank insignia on uniforms, and trinket shops sold knock-off Ronson lighters sporting troopers' unit crests and jump wings. Watches were both plentiful and exotic with lots of unfathomable features and stems, although they usually stopped working after the first heavy rain.

The largest and certainly the busiest part of town was known as "Sin City," a newly constructed, secured compound consisting of about 50 bars that sported such exotic names as the Texas Bar and Grill, the Golden Gate Lounge, and the Mardi Gras Club. Even though they were all identical except for the names, each boasted a

"Sin city" was the busiest part of An Khe

long wooden bar with stools, several tables each, and a couple of chairs. Four or five girls were always there to sell local beer the troops called "tiger piss," and be available for what was referred to as "boom boom." Many young Air Cav troopers fell to the siren's call of "GI, you come with me, I love you long time and too much. We make number one beaucoup boom boom!" Trips to the village were infrequent for troops in the combat units, but the rear area types who never left base camp apparently were able to keep Sin City operational and prosperous in their absence.

The Replacements

Someone once said that the result of combat was the attrition of rifle companies. When A Company landed on the beach at Qui Nhon in September 1965, the company roster listed 156 men and officers present for duty. "When I reported for duty to A Company in November," recalls Specialist Garry Bowles, "the unit was down to fewer than 90 men. Six had been killed, 18 had been wounded, more than 30 were in the hospital with malaria, and 16 had returned stateside for discharge, their enlistments completed. I arrived from the 101st Airborne Division at Fort Campbell,

Specialist Garry Bowles Kentucky, where I had served for about a year after graduating from jump school. I was assigned to A Company, 2nd Battalion (Airborne), 8th Cavalry, as a combat medic. Since I was the ranking specialist in terms of time in grade, I was appointed to be the senior aid man for A Company. I was responsible for the supervision of the other four company medics, each of whom was assigned to a platoon. The medic's job was to make sure that the men in his platoon were healthy and as fit for duty as possible. When a platoon was under enemy fire, it was the medic's job to provide aid to the wounded. A trooper wounded in combat would holler, 'Medic!' and, invariably, one would start crawling to him under enemy fire to provide aid. When a unit has been pushing through the bush for hours on end and the company halted for a rest break, the troopers set up in defensive positions, took a rest, ate a little chow, and unwound a bit.

Not the medic, he's up and down the column, checking for foot blisters, passing out salt tablets, checking cuts on arms and legs caused by the sharp jungle razor grass, treating heat stroke, and taking temperatures of suspected malaria cases. After a firefight, when the guns stop blazing and the smoke had cleared, the medic was still on the job working on the wounded trying to keep guys alive until the medevacs arrived, tagging the dead for evacuation and preparing casualty and status reports for the company commander and platoon leaders. It was a big responsibility, and all of the medics took it very seriously.

A couple of weeks after my arrival in the country, the A Company Commander, Captain McElroy, told me a new medic would be arriving with that afternoon's resupply ship. I stood on the LZ late that afternoon waiting for the helicopter. As the sound of the approaching chopper could be heard, someone popped a smoke grenade to guide it to our location. The Huey landed, and the crew chief started to kick out boxes of ammo, rations, and various other types of supplies and equipment. Three troopers jumped off the hovering Huey as it started to rev up for takeoff. One of the replacements was a good buddy from my 101st Airborne days, Specialist Bobby Lee Elkins, and he walked toward me smiling. It was a wonderful reunion and it was great to see his smiling face. The two other troopers were replacements right out of jump school.

Replacements arriving in country at Ton Son Nhut in Saigon

Lieutenant Bill Marr,
3rd Platoon leader

They were both real big guys.

Private First Class Alex 'Bud' Dziekonski from the Bronx was well over 6 feet and must have weighed at least 220 pounds. He still had lots of stateside fat. The other guy was Private First Class Mike Friedrichs, a big blond kid from Texas. I remember thinking he looked like a pro football player. I hurried them off the LZ to the company command post where Captain McElroy instructed me to take Dziekonski to Lieutenant Taylor at the mortar platoon, and take Friedrichs and Elkins to Lieutenant Bill Marr of the 3rd Platoon.

It was getting dark as we crept around the night defensive perimeter finding the new guys their platoons. When we got to the 3rd Platoon I hung around with Bobby for a while as he brought me up to date on all the news from Fort Campbell. More replacements

Replacements arriving in the bush by supply chopper

began trickling into A Company. The brass was obviously fattening us up for something big. In December Specialist Jim Rockwell was assigned to A Company. Jim was a seasoned soldier who had just arrived from the 101st at Fort Campbell.

The first time I met Jim was at base camp. I noticed he was still wearing the 101st shoulder patch, so I introduced myself as a fellow Screaming Eagle. As we talked, Jim asked what the strange odor was that seemed to envelop the base camp. I explained that they were burning off the latrine cans with aviation fuel.

'Say again,' responded Rockwell in astonishment.

I explained that under each seat in the latrine was a 50-gallon drum that had been cut in half. Obviously these cans would

Jim Rockwell arrives for Fort Campbell

eventually fill and the contents would have to be disposed of; the best solution so far was to burn the contents. You simply roll the can out from under the latrine, then pour aviation gas in the can,

Keep the home fires burning

and light it. After a while you had to stir the smoldering mass with an ax handle to make sure it was burning thoroughly. You had to repeat the process several times to complete the job. Latrine duty was considered punishment duty, so if you keep your nose clean, you'll only have to endure the odor. Jim seemed appreciative of my advice."

"Unlike soldiers of previous wars," reflects Lieutenant Ed Polonitza, "and even some of my comrades in the 1st Cavalry Division, whose journey to the battlefield took weeks or months aboard a troop ship, my trip to Vietnam was quick and relatively comfortable onboard a Pan American commercial flight. Brief stops in Hawaii and Clark Air Force Base in the Philippines gave us a last taste of the real world before the final leg of our flight into Saigon. Everyone on the flight was a replacement, bound for one of the combat units currently fighting the escalating war in Vietnam.

As we approached our landing at Ton Son Nhut Airfield, the plane became eerily quiet. I and my fellow passengers were thinking about the year ahead of us. As I walked across the tarmac at Ton Son Nhut, my most immediate reaction was to the intense heat and glaring sun that beat down mercilessly. The extreme climate of the country would prove to be one of the infantryman's worst enemies. My second reaction was to a huge stack of long rectangular boxes piled neatly on the side of the runway. Some of my fellow passengers noted the same thing. As we approached closer to the stack, we realized these were coffins of dead Americans awaiting shipment back home for burial. Some of us were probably replacing these fallen soldiers. Although my first few minutes in Vietnam were not the most uplifting, in a sense they were a perfect metaphor for the year ahead.

In January 1966, I was reassigned from the 82nd Airborne Division at Fort Bragg, North Carolina, to the 1st Cavalry Division (Airmobile). The 1st Cav's base camp was located at An Khe, a small village about 300 miles north of Saigon. The previous fall, the NVA began a strategic offensive designed to attack across the Central Highlands of South Vietnam and penetrate down Highway 19 that ran from the Cambodian border on the west to the South China Sea on the east. If successful, the Communists would gain control of a major staging area for further attacks against the population centers of South Vietnam.

Our job in the 1st Cav was to eliminate this offensive threat and destroy the North Vietnamese forces pouring across the Cambodian border. When I reached An Khe, I was pleased to be assigned to the Division's 1st Airborne Brigade. This unit was the successor to the 11th Air Assault Division that had been testing the Army's new concepts of airmobile warfare at Fort Benning, Georgia. It was the 1st Cavalry Division's only paratrooper brigade, so I felt lucky when I was assigned to A Company, 2nd Battalion (Airborne), 8th Cavalry. My luck held out, and, when I reported to A Company, I was assigned as the 3rd Platoon leader. As an Airborne Ranger first lieutenant, this was a dream come true. During my assignment with the 82nd Airborne, I had participated in the U.S. invasion of the Dominican Republic where we threw out a Communist group attempting to take control of the country after a vicious civil war. So I had some previous combat experience, but from the stories I heard about the North Vietnamese Infantry, my Dom Rep experience was going to be a piece of cake by comparison. I had no sooner arrived when we were alerted that the entire brigade would move into the field for the biggest campaign of the war to date."

As the Christmas and New Year's holidays approached, the company was kept pretty close to base camp, enjoying a great holiday barbecue right before Christmas and a New Year's Eve party with free beer. But the good times were not to last.

Nicholas Cucci drinking a beer, Jake Townsend facing
camera and Goldsmith far right partying on New Year's

V
Operation Masher/White Wing
First big campaign of 1966

GOOD LUCK
TO OUR
NO.I PONY SOLDIER

Lieutenant Colonel John Hemphill

Men of the 1st Air Cavalry Division moved to the field January 25, 1966, and began the New Year by launching the largest operation thus far in the Vietnam War, Masher/White Wing. After 41 days of continuous action, First Team soldiers shifted their operations to Happy Valley, near their base camp at An Khe and then to the high plateau area near Pleiku and the Cambodian border. Thus, in the period encompassing the first four months of 1966, the "Flying Horsemen" operated in areas from the Cambodian border to the South China Sea, a feat that Major General Harry W.O. Kinnard declares "could not be accomplished by any other divisional unit in the United States Army."

Just before departure, the battalion was assigned a new commander in the person of Lieutenant Colonel John Hemphill, from Division HQ where he was the G-3 responsible for division operations and training. He earned his combat spurs in the Korean War and was as tough as nails. He also wore a Ranger tab over his Airborne tab, and that was reassuring to us rank-and-file troopers. He looked like a leader and talked like a leader. Over the next several months, the soldiers of the 2nd Battalion (Airborne), 8th Cavalry, adopted the nickname, "Hemphill's Humpers." During Operation Masher/White Wing, A Company always seemed to be moving a bit faster and a bit further than the other companies in the battalion, which prompted Captain Tom Forman, after a couple of grueling days of pushing through the jungle, to comment dryly that the Alpha Raiders were the hardiest of all of Hemphill's Humpers. The troopers agreed, and everyone took some pride in the fact that the nickname was respected throughout the division.

Paddy Fight

The Fertile An Lao Valley

During February 1966 the troopers of A Company, 2nd Battalion (Airborne), 8th Cavalry, were conducting combat operations in the An Lao Valley, where the high green mountains sloped gradually to the fertile valley floor. Acre after acre of interlocking rice paddies were fed by the An Lao River and its many tributaries. The valley was lush with vegetation and produced an abundant rice crop. It was the rice that brought the NVA to the An Lao Valley, and the NVA who brought the 1st Air Cavalry.

Conducting Ground Reconnaissance

Searching for signs of the enemy

On the morning of February 23, A Company was conducting combat sweeps through several small villages, which were located amongst the acres of rice paddies and tree lines in our area of operation. The 3rd Platoon, led by Lieutenant Ed Polonitza, had been assigned to provide infantry support to an element of the 1st of the 9th Cavalry.

Recalls Lieutenant Polonitza, "My 3rd Platoon was placed under the operational control of the 1st of the 9th Cavalry that morning. We were assigned the mission of performing ground reconnaissance with one of the 9th Cav's scout helicopter units, which operated with red, white, and blue teams. Red signified the helicopter gun ships, white signified the aerial scouts, and blue was the ground recon unit. On that day we were operational as the blue team. I found this mission to be very irritating and difficult. We were used to being given general operating parameters and then free to act as we saw fit within those parameters. The 9th Cav operated with its scout helicopter essentially as our 'point man,' directing virtually every move we made on the ground. After a very frustrating morning, we were relieved of attachment and ordered to rejoin the rest of A Company, which was doing a search mission through some villages and rice paddy areas looking for enemy units thought to be operating in the area.

Encountering Enemy Sniper Fire

We moved through a densely wooded area running parallel to a rice paddy. The company was several kilometers away from us. We began to take sniper fire as we approached the rest of A Company. Specialist Frank Goldsmith went down with a severe hip wound. At about the same time, Captain James Detrixhe, our company commander, reported that the company was under heavy automatic weapons fire and needed us to reinforce it as soon as we could. We called a medevac helicopter to evacuate Specialist Goldsmith and had to hold in place until the medevac arrived. Captain Detrixhe's radio calls to me became more frantic and impatient. He was in big trouble and needed us. As soon as Goldsmith was medevaced, we moved fast. The enemy fire became more intense. AK-47 rounds were hitting all around us and snapping branches off the trees.

NVA machine gun crew

Crossing the Rice Paddy

By the time we linked up with the company, the enemy fire had died down, and it appeared the North Vietnamese had pulled out. We began crossing the rice paddy to search the areas where the automatic weapons fire had been coming from. Part of the company had crossed the paddy when the wood line exploded with machine gun fire. Specialist Mike Friedrichs and Sergeant Ken Johnson fell into the rice paddy with gunshot wounds.

Lieutenant Ed Polonitza,
3rd Platoon leader

I had just reached the far side of the rice paddy along with the first few 3rd Platoon members when the firing began. The rest of the platoon was pinned down in the rice paddy. I turned around and ran back into the paddy to help bring some return fire against the enemy position. Sergeant Isaac Guest yelled at me to get down behind the dike before I got shot.

I landed in the mud of the rice paddy next to Sergeant Johnson. The blood from his wound was turning the water and muck red. No one could move, as the fire from the tree line became more intense. I told Sergeant Johnson to hang on; we would wait until nightfall and pull him out under cover of darkness. I don't know if this gave him any encouragement or not.

Fighting the Enemy

As we lay in the paddy sludge, I could see Captain Detrixhe and Lieutenant Erle Taylor, the company executive officer, talking on the radio. All of a sudden a flight of helicopter gun ships appeared overhead and started smoking the tree line with rockets. They made run after run pounding the enemy positions. We could feel the enemy fire decreasing in intensity. We knew we had a chance to pull our wounded guys out of the paddy under the cover of the gun ships. Covering one another, we made it to the tree line on the edge of the rice paddy. Everyone was covered with muck, soaking wet, bloody from gunshot wounds, or from the blood-sucking leeches that infested the rice paddy."

Specialist Garry Bowles was the senior company aid man and usually traveled with the company command post in the line of march. The 2nd Platoon medic had been evacuated with malaria the previous day, so Bowles was filling in until a replacement arrived:

"It was a little past noon, recalls Bowles, "and I was with the 2nd

Senior Alpha Medic Garry Bowles

Platoon, as they advanced parallel of a small river. It was a beautiful day; the sky was a perfect blue without a single cloud in sight. There was a cool breeze blowing across my face, and I can remember thinking how good it felt. It was what soldiers for a thousand years have called 'A Walk in the Sun.' As our column moved forward, I noticed a sandbar running down the center of the river. I waded across onto the sandbar thinking it would be fun to walk there for a while. As soon as I had reached it, I heard lots of automatic weapons fire in the distance. The troopers on the bank of the river immediately hit the ground with their weapons at the ready. Suddenly I felt very stupid standing there fully exposed in the middle of that river.

I sloshed back across to the safety of the riverbank as fast as I could. Reaching dry land, I ran for the nearest cover I could find and landed next to the platoon radiotelephone operator, Bill Garlinger. He had his radio handset pressed hard to his ear. I could hear lots of excit-

"Paddy Fight" (c) George Cook

ed voices coming from his radio. Garlinger yelled to Lieutenant Gill Cochran who was about five meters in front of him, 'Sir, 3rd Platoon has enemy contact and the head of the column is also taking fire! The Captain wants to talk to you!' Bill crawled forward on his belly extending the radio handset to the platoon leader.

As Lieutenant Cochran excitedly talked to the Captain, the platoon sergeant, a big guy named Carerra, came running down the trail and dove for cover between Garlinger and Cochran. The Lieutenant, still holding his handset to his ear, began talking and rapidly gesturing to Sergeant Carerra and pointing up the column. The platoon sergeant then got to his feet and started running forward. Lieutenant Cochran then yelled to the troopers behind him, 'Saddle up and move out!' We moved forward at a trot, entering into a wide rice paddy that was to the left of our line of march.

Sergeant Carerra was there as we arrived and was busy placing the platoon on line for an assault across the paddy. As we got into position for our attack, I watched mortar crew members set up their tube for a fire mission. They placed the bottom of the tube in the base plate, but when they laid the gun in its supporting bipod, it immediately sank in the mud.

One of the mortar crew members, a big guy by the name of Dziekonski, kneeled down in the mud facing the gun. The crew placed the tube on his shoulder for support, and Specialist Richardson fired several quick rounds that landed very close to the enemy posi-

Attacking across the paddy under enemy fire

tions. It was an incredible feat considering they were firing without the bipod or aiming mechanism. We began our assault, and like the mortar crew before, fell victim to the mud. Troopers were sinking up to their knees in the muck, bringing the attack to a standstill. Individual troopers then began jumping on to the dikes, and, fully exposed, started running toward the enemy positions, firing their weapons as they advanced.

The entire platoon followed suit. I remember as I ran forward across the dikes, bullets impacted in the water all around me as I experienced a curious sense of exhilaration.

We made good progress until about halfway across. The enemy had apparently gauged our range, and we ran into a withering wall of automatic weapons fire. We all immediately jumped from the dikes into the paddy, seeking cover. All along the dikes, troopers began returning fire as best they could. As I lay there in the mud firing my M-16, I thought to myself, 'What had begun that day as a walk in the sun' had definitely taken a turn for the worse.'"

Specialist Juan Fernandez was a rifleman with the 3rd Platoon and recalls the march back to rejoin A Company, fighting its way past enemy infested tree lines and across flooded rice paddies. "I remember coming around a hill and noticed to my left an M-60 machine gun crew setting up to cover our assault. They began to lay down covering fire as we quickly spread out on line for our attack across the paddy. Halfway across, our advance was slowed, as many of us began

Rice paddies covered the floor of the An Lao Valley

sinking in the mud. Helping one another, we advanced under fire to where we found a stream. We crossed it and continued up the side of its bank, which looked down on the enemy village.

Huey gunship pounds enemy position

We started down the other side of the bank, the entire platoon firing into the enemy positions that had been firing at us. As our fire increased, the enemy's fire slackened and eventually ended entirely. Apparently, they did not want to stick around. We cleared the enemy positions and proceeded across the rice paddy. Walking in single file and thinking the enemy had enough, we were all laughing and joking. Our laughter quickly ended as we heard gunfire. The water around me started to dance from the impacting rounds. The term 'Get down!' had a whole new meaning that day, as we all jumped into the rice paddy for cover behind a dike. They say in a firefight any cover is good cover, but the dike offered too little protection for my liking. As we were laying in the paddy mud and water, I saw Sergeant Ken Johnson rise from behind the dike and fire a light antitank rocket into the enemy position. As I watched the rocket leave its tube, Sergeant Johnson fell forward on the dike, badly wounded in the leg. Several of his men, fearing he would get hit again, rushed forward to pull him off the exposed dike and provided him medical aid.

As I was firing from a prone position behind the dike, the mud and paddy water made it difficult to reload my M-16. I remember seeing rounds hit the water all around me as I lay as flat as possible behind my cover. We were all pinned down, and, at that point, unable to move forward or backward; there was nowhere to go, so we all fired back from the cover of the dike as best we could. Then, all of a sudden you could hear the wop, wop, and wop of helicopters blades. I'm sure I wasn't the only one to experience the thrill of seeing those beautiful helicopter gun ships pulling in behind us.

They fired their rockets over our heads and pounded the enemy positions. It was then that someone yelled for us to pull back across the paddy. We all knew what to do and how to do it.

"Carrying our wounded, we leapfrogged back across the paddy with each fire team taking its turn so as not run over each other in all that mud. As we pulled back across the paddy, the gun ships continued to smoke the enemy positions. The machine gun team that had covered our assault across the paddy was burning up, its barrel providing suppressing fire for our withdrawal. We all got back to our original starting point. Everyone was exhausted and soaked with water and mud. Sergeant Guest came over to where I was laying on my back catching my breath. He looked down at me and asked if I had been shot. I was covered with blood. 'No,' I replied, 'damn leeches got me.' I was covered with them."

Crawling to Safety

Mike Friedrichs,
3rd Platoon rifleman

Mike Friedrichs remembers, "I kept popping my head up to see where the enemy fire was coming from. Juan Fernandez kept screaming at me to keep down. I found a target and started returning fire with my M-16. After a few rounds my weapon malfunctioned, a broken extractor. I then began to arm my LAW to return fire. I was almost ready to launch my rocket when I felt this horrible numbness and burning from my waist to my toes. I rolled over on my back. I knew I had been hit. At first I didn't want to look. Thinking the worst, I reached down and was relieved to find everything was intact. Two troopers helped me out of my gear, and our medic, Bobby Elkins, crawled over, and put a pressure bandage on my wound. An AK-47 round had entered my left hip and passed through both legs."

Two of my buddies started to drag me out of the rice paddy, but the pain of being dragged was too much, plus the three of us bunched up in the paddy offered the enemy an excellent target. I told them to get behind a dike, and give me covering fire, and I would crawl out of the paddy myself. I was still receiving fire all

around me; the enemy still had my range. I could see the impacting bullets spitting up
mud as I backstroked
across the paddy using
rice shoots to pull
myself through the
muck. My legs were
useless. When I got to a
dike I had to cross, I
would get as close as I
could, wait for the
enemy fire to subside,
and then roll over the
rice paddy dike.
Troopers at the edge of
the paddy were giving

*The enemy would attack, fall back,
and then attack again*

me covering fire. They were also cheering me on as I pulled myself
to safety. I can still recall Sergeant Guest, firing his M-16 and
yelling profanities at the enemy while encouraging me back to the
safety of the 3rd Platoon lines.

*Lieutenant Erle Taylor,
A Company XO*

Platoons Under Fire

1st Lieutenant Erle Taylor was
the A Company executive officer and
recalled spending most of the afternoon
on the radio coordinating fire and
maneuver against the enemy, who
would appear, then disappear, only to
appear again. On February 23, 1966, A
Company was conducting search and
destroy missions with elements of our
battalion's D Company. We were moving from map coordinate Bird up the
western side of the river to coordinate
Cord. It was about 1300 hours when
Lieutenant Polonitza reported by radio
that his 3rd Platoon was under fire. At
that time the lead elements of the A
Company column also came under fire.
The 2nd Platoon under Lieutenant

Cochran was ordered forward to attack across the rice paddy with the support of one of our mortar teams.

After moving 200 meters across the paddy, the 2nd Platoon came under intense automatic weapons fire from several different locations. Artillery and mortar fire were brought to bear on the

Dustoff arrives to extract the wounded

enemy positions, as the 2nd Platoon continued its advance under the barrage. The position was seized by 2nd Platoon, but no enemy soldiers were found. The 2nd Platoon then received fire from its left flank, and fire support was directed to the new enemy positions. Lieutenant Polonitza's 3rd Platoon continued to the Northwest sweeping the village and the tree line, while continually drawing enemy fire. We then deployed to map position Moi Nhon in the vicinity of coordinate Cord. There, we found a farmer who said there had been about 50 Viet Cong who had been shadowing us from the tree lines and attacking our line of march. It appeared that they were acting as a delaying force against the A Company advance. Once again the enemy broke contact and was nowhere to be found. We were then ordered to return to a predetermined map coordinate. When we were a couple of hundred meters from the position, we once again came under enemy fire from all locations previously mentioned. The enemy fire was extremely accurate and very intense. Once again we called in mortars and artillery, and, for good measure, gun ships, which pounded the area with rockets. The D Company recon platoon then attacked the enemy in an attempt to roll up their flank. The recon platoon met with stiff resistance and suffered high casualties.

Mortar crews began pounding the area with white phosphorous and, after dropping about 20 rounds on the positions, the enemy fire ceased. A Company then covered the withdrawal of D Company to the friendly tree line where we evacuated our wounded. We then were extracted to location Bird, arriving about 2000 hours that night. It had been a very long day."

Killed in Action

As the paratroopers of A Company were preparing for extraction, Private First Class Thomas Jay Oglethorpe of Petaluma, California, was excitedly showing off a bullet hole in his helmet. Specialist Rockwell recalled that everyone was kidding Tom about being the luckiest guy in A Company. The next day, February 24, Private First Class Oglethorpe, along with five other A Company troopers, were killed while counterattacking an enemy ambush. Private First Class Oglethorpe was 17 years of age; he was killed in action 10 days short of his 18th birthday.

Private First Class Thomas Jay Oglethorpe

Ambush at An Lao

It had been six very long weeks since the battalion had left base camp in the Central Highlands of Vietnam. For the past month and a half troopers had humped their butts to the bone. Everyone was tired and a bit edgy. They'd been in daily enemy contact for about a week---nothing major---just a lot of small skirmishes. Although our casualties had been light, we definitely knew we were in Indian country.

Surprise NVA Attack

A Company's senior combat medic, Specialist Garry Bowles, recalls, "It was about 0900 on the morning of February 24 when we air assaulted to the crest of a small mountain. Our mission was to move down a series of spiny little ridges leading to the floor of the valley below. It was just another day in the bush. We'd done it a hundred times before.

The company moved down the ridgeline in a two-column formation, the point men hacking a path with their machetes for the troops bringing up the rear. We had been beating the bush for about four hours when suddenly automatic weapons fire erupted

Lieutenants Polonitza and Cochran

on our left flank. The 2nd Platoon under the command of Lieutenant Gill Cochran reported making contact with an enemy squad. The 2nd Platoon captured two NVA soldiers, along with a carriage-mounted machine gun, ammunition, five rucksacks, and assorted enemy documents, and reported moving in pursuit of a fleeing enemy soldier. Within minutes of the 2nd Platoon contact, Lieutenant Polonitza, commanding the 3rd Platoon, radioed hearing voices on his left flank and led his men in an assault that killed five of the enemy, captured a second carriage-mounted machine gun and ammunition, a cache of 81mm mortar shells, plus assorted enemy equipment. It was becoming more and more obvious to everyone that we were nipping at the heels of a significant North Vietnamese infantry outfit. The company moved forward in pur-

B40 Rocket Launcher penetrates 12-inch armor plate

Private First Class
Dick Marshall

suit of the enemy and was immediately met with intense automatic weapons, machine gun, and recoilless rifle fire; the point man and three other A Company troopers were killed instantly. Captain James Detrixhe rushed forward in a crouch to the point of contact. Private First Class Dick Marshall, his radio operator, and I were hot on his heels. I moved forward behind the Captain noticing troopers on both our flanks firing into the jungle."

As Lieutenant Polonitza remembers, "We approached a small clearing toward our left flank. The front element of our column led by our 'point man,' Specialist Leonard Lawrence, guided our platoon around the side of the clearing. I was near the front of our formation, behind a fire team and a machine gun crew. As we skirted the clearing, all hell broke loose on the lower left flank of our column. The clearing erupted with automatic weapons fire and rocket-propelled grenades tearing through our column at very close range. The 2nd Platoon, on our left flank, and the remainder of my 3rd Platoon, were immediately pinned down and suffering heavy casualties from the point-blank enemy fire. At this point, our platoons were fighting for their lives."

Specialist Bowles vividly recalls, "I suddenly found myself, along with Marshall and the Captain, in front of the column; we had advanced beyond our lines into a small jungle clearing. Everything seemed to happen simultaneously. I couldn't distinguish the blinking muzzle flashes from the growl of automatic weapons fire that was coming at me from the far edge of the clearing. I could hear the screams of men wounded in that initial fusillade. It was as if some great evil beast had reached up from the bowels of the earth to capture everyone in the clearing in its angry grip of terror and fear. The shock of the moment filled every fiber of my being with a paralyzing numbness. It was as if I was one with all that was swirling around me. All that ever was and all that ever would be was happening to me in that split second of time."

Second Barrage of Enemy Fire

It was February 24, 1966, and somewhere in the An Lao Valley Republic of Vietnam, A Company, 2nd Battalion (Airborne), 8th Cavalry, had just walked dead into a hornet's nest of NVA infantry. "As the impact of the initial NVA barrage of fire subsided," recalls Bowles, "My sense of time and awareness slowly returned. I could hear troopers to my rear return fire into the tree line. I could hear American voices, some barking commands, some crying for help. Directly in front of me, in the small jungle clearing, lay several dead paratroopers. At the edge of the clearing, Captain Detrixhe, was behind a small knoll, firing his M-16 on full automatic into the tree line. Dick Marshall, was hugging the ground about 10 feet to the left of me. Suddenly Marshall sprang to his feet and made a rush to the knoll and safety. The radio on his back, with its big whip antenna sticking a couple of feet in the air, made Dick a perfect target for the NVA gunners. Several bursts hit Dick, throwing him to the ground. There was a loud pop and a bright white flame, followed by swirling red smoke. An enemy tracer round had ignited a smoke grenade dangling from Dick's web gear. The billowing smoke enveloped the clearing with a dense red fog that was filled with hundreds of small whirlpools caused by the automatic weapons fire coming from both sides of the clearing. I took a deep breath and sprinted into the smoke to where I thought Dick had fallen. I found him lying on his back, shot several times in the chest and stomach. The flame from the exploding grenade had set his uniform on fire, burning him severely from the hip down to his knee. I quickly beat the smoldering flames with my left hand as I poured water on him with the canteen in my right hand. Dick had a funny blue pallor to his face; he had swallowed lots of smoke and was having a hard time trying to breathe.

I crooked his head backward over my left arm and cleared his throat, and then slowly trickled water into his mouth. He coughed up a mouthful of red mucus. I didn't know if it was blood or just red smoke that he had coughed up with the water. Dick was badly hurt, and my first thought was to drag him to the safety of the knoll where Captain Detrixhe was firing. I jumped up, grabbed Dick by the back of his shoulder harness, and started to drag him backward to the knoll. It was like a dream, and I was moving in slow motion; no matter how hard or fast I tried to move, it seemed like I really wasn't going anywhere. I was literally frozen in time as AK-47 rounds whizzed past my face. The medical bag that was slung over my shoulder dropped to the ground, the straps cut in two by enemy fire. Suddenly I felt my right thigh and it was wet. I looked down to see that my canteen had been shredded by rifle fire. It was water soaking my leg, not blood, thank God! Dick's body convulsed as several more rounds impacted his torso. I suddenly fell backward over the sloping knoll, letting go of Dick as I fell. The impact of the fall freed me from my dreamlike state, and I lay flat on my back watching tracer rounds fly over my head. I was safe behind the slope. I quickly rolled over on my belly and crawled forward to grab Dick's shoulder harness in order to pull him to safety. Captain Detrixhe reached over and grabbed Dick's other shoulder harness, and together, we pulled him over the edge of the slope. Captain Detrixhe put a fresh magazine into his weapon and lifted to his knee to pour more fire into the tree line. His body suddenly lifted up and spun in mid air. He landed on his back, facing me, but his helmet and the top of his head were both missing. He slumped to one side with blood pumping from what was left of his head spraying my face in a sticky mist. I reached over to Dick's wrist feeling for a pulse; there was none.

I lay here between the Captain and Dick, trying to stay perfectly still, fearing that any movement I made would attract enemy fire. Over the din of weapons fire, I could hear someone calling out to me, Bowles recalled, 'Doc, Doc!' It was Lieutenant Erle Taylor, the company XO. I yelled back to him while trying not to move, 'Taylor, you're now 6, you're now 6.'

The number 6 was the common radio designation for a company commander. I was trying to tell him that the CO was dead, and he was now in charge of the company.

He hollered back 'I copy that, hang on!'

What else could I do? I continued to hug the ground for dear life. To the left of the clearing, a crescendo of weapons fire erupted. It sounded like M-16s. Based on where the firing was coming from, I figured it must be Ed Polonitza's 3rd Platoon flanking the enemy positions in the tree line."

As Lieutenant Polonitza recalls, "At this point, I was about 10 to 15 meters from the center of the enemy force. I felt the best option was for us to flank the enemy ambush from their rear. A small group of us, including my RTO, Specialist Sid Shearing; Specialist Leonard Lawrence; Dave Dement; Jake Townsend; and Dwight Lamsom, an M-60 machine gunner; along with Nick Cucci,

Machine gunners Lamsom and Cucci

his assistant gunner, began to crawl around the NVA flank. As we maneuvered forward, we began to receive incoming rounds from the rest of A Company, who were firing through the enemy positions.

When I felt that we were behind the enemy, Shearing radioed Lieutenant Taylor, who had assumed command after Captain Detrixhe's death, and requested that the rest of the company hold their fire as we made our assault to eliminate the enemy position. We attacked directly into a small group of NVA infantrymen, pouring fire into their position. I threw a hand grenade toward the enemy position. The grenade hit a tree limb between our small group and the NVA and exploded harmlessly. At this point we were attacking the enemy from both their front and rear. The NVA infantrymen, realizing they were being surrounded,

3rd Platoon flanks the enemy

fled, dropping their equipment as they ran. Unfortunately for them, they ran directly into Charlie Company of our battalion, which was moving to reinforce us. The fight was over. Then began the sad and mournful business of collecting swollen gray bodies of our dead and carrying them back to that jungle clearing for which they had died. It was a difficult day, a tough day, a day which none who were there will ever forget."

"As I lay in the clearing hugging the ground for dear life," Bowles recalls, "I could hear the roar of gunfire gradually subsiding into the occasional pop, pop of M-16s firing single shots. I looked to my rear as I heard American voices approaching. Crouching troopers with weapons at the ready were emerging from the jungle into the clearing from all sides. The weapons fire had subsided and had been replaced with the excited chatter of voices all around me. I heard someone say 'You all right Doc?'

I looked up; it was Lieutenant Taylor, his arm outstretched offering to help me to my feet. I took his hand and grunted as he pulled me upright. My legs were like rubber and I felt sick to my stomach.

'Yeah,' I said, 'I'm fine.'

'A platoon is moving up to secure the clearing,' said Taylor. 'They've got chain saws to knock down some of these trees. We'll be able to bring in some medevacs as soon as they're finished, so have

Medic Bobby Elkins

your medics collect all the wounded as close to the edge of the LZ as possible.'

I shook my head in response.

He lowered his voice and said, 'I'll have a squad start gathering the dead. You can evacuate them after we get the wounded out.'"

'Yes sir,' I replied, suddenly feeling even sicker to my stomach.

Two of the platoon medics, Bobby Elkins and Private First Class Mike Huggins, appeared from out of the jungle, each helping wounded troopers. Soldiers carrying the seriously wounded in makeshift litters fashioned from ponchos followed them.

Elkins, over the grrrrr of the chainsaws, hollered to me from the

Evacuating the wounded

edge of the now expanding LZ, 'Where are we setting up the aid station?'

'Right where you are!' I hollered back as I walked toward him.

Within 10 minutes a half dozen more wounded arrived at the aid station. We patched them up as best we could and filled out medevac tags so the evac hospital would know what treatment we had provided. Several of the troopers died before we heard the whomp, whomp, whomp of the approaching choppers. We rushed to load the most severely wounded onto the first chopper. It no sooner lifted off from the LZ than the second chopper landed and we repeated the process. There wasn't the same sense of urgency for the dead, and since nightfall was quickly approaching, it was decided our dead would be lifted out in the morning, along with several wounded enemy soldiers captured in our final assault.

There was no rush. Just as I had done with the wounded, I made a list of the names of the dead troopers to be evacuated. Many of the names were all too familiar. A platoon sergeant by the name of Carerra walked over and asked me if I had seen Lieutenant Taylor.

'Over there,' I said, pointing to the makeshift command post at the other end of the LZ. 'Give him this,' I said, 'It's the names of the dead and wounded.'

'How many?' he asked.

I shrugged my shoulders, and replied, 'Don't know.'

He shook his head as if he understood and taking the list from my hand, he strode off toward the CP.

I sat down next to Bobby and Mike. None of us spoke. There were no words for how we felt, and we were just too exhausted for idle talk. We sat in silence, with our hands, faces, and uniforms covered in the blood of our comrades, each of us replaying the events of the day over and over in our minds.

It was just before dusk when we got the word that a resupply chopper was inbound to our position. The chopper arrived and hovered about 10 feet off the ground. The door gunner kicked out a cargo of food, ammo, water, and medical supplies. I stood there watching as the chopper started to lift off for its return flight to base camp. The chopper slowly gained altitude as it flew past me, and I saw the gunner

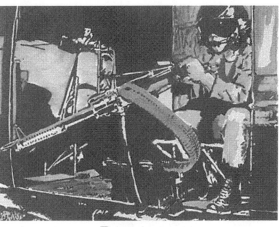

Door gunner
(c) George Cook

look down and wave. I stood there in that terrible place and waved back, wishing with all my soul that I could leave also."

Sergeant Garry O.
Bowles

Cited For Heroism

This article appeared in the *Daily Kennebec Journal,* Augusta Maine, April 1966.

"Word has been received here that Sergeant Garry O. Bowles, 1st Cavalry Division, (Airmobile) U.S. Army, has been awarded the Bronze Star Medal with 'V' device, for heroism.

Sergeant Bowles is the son of Colonel (Ret.) and Mrs. George M. Bowles, Treasure Island, Florida. He is a graduate of Cony High School and makes his home with his aunt, Miss Ellen Cunningham, 122 Sewall Street."

The citation read, in part, "Specialist Four Bowles distinguished himself by heroism while serving as a company aid man in the vicinity of the An Lao Valley, Republic of Vietnam on February 24, 1966. When contact was made with an enemy force, the company headquarters group moved to the front, near the point of contact. A sniper at close range hit the commander and one of his radio operators. The sniper struck the radio operator's pistol belt, causing a smoke grenade to go off and burn him. Specialist Four Bowles rushed from behind his cover to render aid. He succeeded in removing the pistol belt and putting the fire out, and continued treating the radio operator until the smoke lifted, and the sniper again shot the radio operator. The last rounds killed this individual and hit Specialist Four Bowles' equipment. This outstanding display of devotion to duty and personal bravery is in keeping with the highest standards of the military service and reflects a great credit upon himself, his unit, and the United States Army."

The medal was given by direction of President Johnson.

Battle for Hospital Hill

A group of Alpha Raiders pose for a photograph prior to departing for the hills and mountains of the An Lao Valley during Operation Masher/White Wing.

Air Cav grunts in Vietnam typically ate a lot of dirt while humping up and down hills. They fought for hills inch by inch, while pulling themselves upward on their bellies to their summits with all weapons firing on full automatic. Some hills were taken by air assaulting into hilltop clearings that were only big enough to hold a

Taking the hill (c)
Illustrated by George Cook

couple of Hueys at a time. Jumping into a hot LZ under fire while gun ships peppered the perimeter with rocket and machine gunfire is something not easily forgotten. Some hills had no enemy at all except for the hill itself, because soldiers clawed and hacked with their machetes to make a path to the top only to hack their way down the other side. Grunts never kept the hills; only took them. The hills themselves weren't really important; what was important was to show that the NVA couldn't have them. In the immortal words uttered on operation "Nathan Hale" by Ranger Sergeant Duke DuShane, "High ground good, low ground bad."

Follow Me

In 1966, Lieutenant Ed Polonitza was a platoon leader in A Company, 2nd Battalion (Airborne), 8th Cavalry, of the famous 1st Air Cavalry Division. A platoon leader was the first officer an infantry-man encountered in his upward chain of command. To his men he was part coach, part quarterback. All platoon leaders were second or first lieutenants, and, for the most part, they were between 20 to 24 years of age. They ate the same food, walked down the same rain-soaked jungle trails, and experienced the same fears and exhilarations of the grunts they led. The infantry platoon leader had one mission and that was to engage and destroy the enemy. His job description was simple: "Follow me."

Lieutenant Polonitza recalls, "During the month of February 1966, A Company, 2nd Battalion (Airborne), 8th Cavalry, had been conducting search and destroy missions in Binh Dinh Province, which is about 330 miles northeast of Saigon on the South China Sea. Beautiful wide beaches gave way to a coastal plain of fertile rice pad-dies. Water for the paddies flowed from streams and rivers descend-

Humping the bush

ing from mountains and ridges further to the west. These Central Highlands were an infantryman's worst nightmare, tough rugged terrain covered with triple canopy jungle. Throughout the war, those highlands were the background for the brutal struggle between the soldiers of the 1st Cavalry Division and the North Vietnamese regulars who used the mountains as a staging ground for attacks against strategic targets along the coast. We had been in continuous close contact with the North Vietnamese forces and had suffered a number of casualties. On February 24, our company commander, Captain James Detrixhe and several other A Company soldiers had been killed in a fierce firefight.

On February 25, Captain Tom Forman assumed command of A Company. Captain Forman was well-known to the unit. He had commanded the company upon its departure from Fort Benning, Georgia, the previous summer. Captain Forman, a very gregarious, party-loving man, had been relieved of command as the result of some over-exuberance at a bar in Hawaii during a stopover on the trip to Vietnam. An experienced company commander was just what we needed; he was both calm and cool and proved to be a top-notch combat leader over the next six months that I served with him.

Our first significant mission under Captain Forman was to find and destroy an enemy field hospital located in the mountains west of Bong Son. On the morning of February 27, we executed a combat air assault into a landing zone on a mountaintop in the vicinity of the suspected hospital site. As our UH-1 troop-carrying helicopters, 'slicks,' were easy targets for enemy gunners, our goal was to get them in and out of the LZ in a matter of seconds. To do this, the lead trooper on each side of the slick stood on the landing strut and jumped into the LZ while the Huey was 10 to 15 feet in the air. The rest of the squad would swiftly follow him. Frequently the choppers would not have to actually land and could be quickly out of harm's way.

We were heavily loaded with equipment and ammunition as we penetrated into the jungle surrounding the LZ. Most of my platoon soldiers were riflemen who carried and M-16 and 500 rounds of 5.56-

Alpha Raiders Captain
Tom Forman

millimeter ammunition. Each of the three rifle squads had two grenadiers armed with an M-79 grenade launcher and 50 grenades as well as some buckshot rounds for close combat. Our weapons squad had two M-60 machine guns. Each gunner had an assistant loaded down with several thousand rounds. All of us carried fragmentation hand grenades, smoke grenades, claymore mines, c-rations, two canteens of water, bedrolls, and other personal equipment. As we left the LZ, I noticed Captain Forman's bedroll was square in shape as opposed to round like everyone else's. I would find out later what that was all about.

Our intelligence indicated that the hospital was located in a ravine formed by two ridgelines extending out from our landing zone. One platoon probed directly into the ravine while the rest of the company, including my platoon, advanced down the ridgeline above the suspected hospital site.

The heavy jungle limited visibility to just a few yards ahead of the point man and made our advance slow and difficult. That morning was uneventful, but early in the afternoon, a burst of M-16 fire broke the silence of the jungle. Our lead platoon had made contact with several North Vietnamese, killing one.

Almost immediately there was another quick firefight, then another. In each case, the enemy was either killed or ran down a small, but recently used, trail we were following. At about 3 p.m., our advance was stopped by several machine guns delivering accurate fire on the lead platoon. Captain Forman made radio contact with a scout chopper from the 1st of the 9th Cavalry that was over our position. The scout was able to deploy a helicopter gun ship that took out the enemy machine guns, and we moved on.

As it was now obvious that we were in contact with a significant North Vietnamese unit, Captain Forman directed the 1st Platoon, led by Lieutenant Marty Stango, to maneuver to the right in an attempt to outflank the enemy position. Artillery fire pounded all around us to cover our advance. During its flanking movement, the 1st Platoon bumped into the enemy hospital. The 2nd Platoon, led by Lieutenant Gill Cochran, maneuvered quickly in support of the 1st Platoon.

With two platoons on line and my 3rd Platoon in reserve, A Company began its attack on the hospital position. Both platoons encountered a wall of fire from well-concealed bunker positions extending up the side of the ravine. Any further assault into this heavily fortified defense would have resulted in heavy casualties, so the two platoons could only hold their positions and continue the fight.

In an attempt to flank the enemy position, Captain Forman ordered my platoon to attack around the right of the hospital site. We began this assault but encountered heavily fortified bunker positions and intense automatic rifle and machine gun fire.

Our lead squad, led by Sergeant Isaac Guest, had actually advanced into the enemy bunkers before being surrounded by North Vietnamese infantry. Seeing that Sergeant Guest's squad was pinned down and unable to move, the rest of the platoon threw smoke grenades into Sergeant Guest's position, which allowed him to withdraw under cover of the smoke. One of my vivid memories of that day was Sergeant Guest and his squad emerging from a wall of bright yellow, red, green, and white smoke, and back into the relative safety of our position.

At this point, all of A Company was under heavy fire and fully

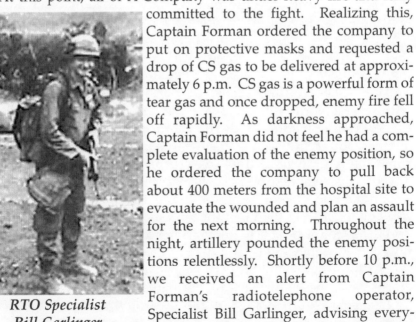 committed to the fight. Realizing this, Captain Forman ordered the company to put on protective masks and requested a drop of CS gas to be delivered at approximately 6 p.m. CS gas is a powerful form of tear gas and once dropped, enemy fire fell off rapidly. As darkness approached, Captain Forman did not feel he had a complete evaluation of the enemy position, so he ordered the company to pull back about 400 meters from the hospital site to evacuate the wounded and plan an assault for the next morning. Throughout the night, artillery pounded the enemy positions relentlessly. Shortly before 10 p.m., we received an alert from Captain Forman's radiotelephone operator, Specialist Bill Garlinger, advising every-

RTO Specialist
Bill Garlinger

one to keep their heads down. An Army Caribou flare ship was inbound to our position for the purpose of illuminating the hill for a napalm strike by carrier-based Navy jets. Shortly after the alert, flares started popping and igniting in the night sky above us.

The hill and surrounding jungle took on an eerie glow as the burning flares drifted slowly to the ground. Garlinger and other members of the CP group fashioned together a half dozen flashlights with red lenses and pointed them skyward in a straight line toward the target. In a further attempt to guide the incoming jets, Garlinger fired a full magazine of M-16 tracer ammunition toward the crest of the hill. Over the sound of the tracer rounds, you could hear the growl of the low-flying Navy F-4 Phantoms approaching our positions, then the loud roar of exploding napalm canisters bursting into sheets of hot white flame against the entrenched enemy. Many of the troopers, exhausted from the day's fight, slept through the attack, too tired to notice. Those who were awake and on watch were too tired to cheer.

Fix Bayonets!

At 5 a.m. the next day, February 28, we moved into position for a frontal attack on the hospital site. Artillery continued to pound the area. My platoon was on the left and 2nd Platoon on the right as we moved into position at the base of the hill ready for the assault. I passed the word to fix bayonets, and the attack began. We attacked abreast and well spread out. Marty Stango's 1st Platoon provided flank and rear security. A short way up the hill, we made our first contact with the fortified enemy positions. We threw grenades or fired directly into each bunker, and one by one, the North Vietnamese bunkers were destroyed. Several of us carried

2nd Platoon leader
Lieutenant Marty Stango

LAWs or light anti-tank weapons; these proved very effective in knocking out the dug-in enemy. For several hundred meters up the side of the ravine, the fight continued. In some instances, our riflemen crawled into the bunkers and ripped the enemy virtually in two with their M-16s firing on full automatic. Specialists Jim Rockwell and Leonard Lawrence teamed up as they assaulted the hill.

Rockwell fired his LAW rockets exploding them against the back of the defended positions. Lawrence rushed forward and finished off the entrenched enemy with automatic weapons fire. They repeated this maneuver as they fought their way up the hill. The defending NVA put up tough resistance, but these two paratroopers of A Company proved themselves far tougher, killing numerous enemy soldiers as they advanced."

Specialist Juan Fernandez, an 18-year-old rifleman, recalls, "I remember moving up the hill in a crouched position, moving from tree to tree and boulder to boulder. Specialists Rockwell and Lawrence were to my left front; Dave Dement and I were slightly behind them. Sergeant Guest was right behind all of us hollering for us to get up that hill. I really wasn't sure what scared us the most, the enemy automatic weapons fire or Sergeant Guest pushing us forward. Once we started to advance, all hell broke loose, and you could see NVA soldiers all over the place. Their heads were popping out of their holes as they fired down on us. We were throwing hand grenades and firing our M-16s at the bunkers as we advanced. Each time we passed a bunker, one of us would unload a magazine into the opening and then move forward, bunker by bunker.

We then advanced to the left and moved into the actual hospital site. The enemy had little huts set up for their wounded, lying inside the huts in what looked like shallow graves. Lawrence and I entered one of the huts to check for booby-traps. A couple of NVA wounded were lying flat on their backs in their holes; they looked terrified. I think they thought we were going to kill them.

Instead, we carried them to the top of the hill where Captain Forman had set up his command post. There, two of our company medics, Garry Bowles and Bobby Elkins, provided them medical aid and fed them some of our famous c-rations. Sergeant Guest then ordered my squad halfway down the slope of the hill to set up defensive positions against a possible enemy counterattack. As we took up our new positions, I thought we were probably as glad as the wounded enemy soldiers were that it was over, and that we would all live to see another day."

Take the Hill!

As 3rd Platoon's attack up the hill began, Specialist Dave Dement was right in the middle of the assault line. Specialist James Trujillo was to his left and Sergeant Guest's squad was to his right. As the attack progressed, Dement and Trujillo would cover one another as they attacked each enemy fortification in their sector. About halfway up the hill, Dement fell down beside an NVA bunker. Trujillo ran up in front of the dugout, pointed his M16 about a yard from Dement's head, and emptied his magazine into the enemy position. Dement covered his ears and called Trujillo some choice names. Trujillo yelled back, "Didn't you see that NVA?" Dement rolled over and saw an NVA soldier down in the dugout, still moving. Trujillo then fired three more rounds into the bunker, each shot lifting the enemy soldier off the ground.

Further up the hill, Dement saw the tip of an enemy AK-47 firing out of a bunker opening. He was afraid to throw a grenade into the fortification for fear of missing the opening and having the grenade roll back down the hill and explode among the charging cavalrymen. The young rifleman was able to crawl close enough to empty a magazine from his M16 into the bunker, neutralizing it. After emptying his magazine, Dement rolled over and began to slide down the hill. As he slid past Sergeant Guest, he heard the tough NCO say, "Dement, what in the hell do you call that?"

Dement responded, "Did you like that, Sarge?"

Sergeant Guest yelled back, "Just keep it moving, and let's take this hill!"

Lieutenant Polonitza recalls that the intensity and ferocity of the attack completely overwhelmed the North Vietnamese: "Having experienced 18 hours of pounding by the 1st Cavalry artillery, the CS drop, napalm strike, and now this well-executed and determined infantry assault, the NVA had had enough. After several hours of fighting, we reached the top of the ridgeline and set up security in the event of a North Vietnamese counter-attack. Captain Forman and the company headquarters group who had been following the lead platoons soon joined us. I will always remember his after-action comments that day. He said he had witnessed the best infantry attack he had seen since leaving Fort Benning. With that, he unrolled his square bedroll and passed around a bottle of Jack Daniels with which we drank a toast to the defeated enemy who had fought courageously if not particularly wisely that day.

A Company's attack on this hospital position resulted in its complete destruction as an enemy stronghold; numerous enemy soldiers were killed, many more were wounded, and we captured large amounts of equipment and supplies. On our side, we had only a few wounded, and, thankfully, no one killed. We enjoyed the payback for our comrades who had fallen in battles over the past month. For the infantrymen of A Company, 2nd Battalion (Airborne), 8th Cavalry, the celebration was short lived. This was just another day in a long year of slogging the jungles of the Central Highland of South Vietnam."

Letter to the Troops

Major General
Harry W. O. Kinnard

Here in a letter from General Harry W. O. Kinnard to his men is the story of the first big campaign of the year, Operation Masher/White Wing:

"We began with operation south of Bong Son on January 25 to increase the security of Route 1 and to confuse the enemy as to which way we were headed. Then on January 28, D-Day for Operation Masher, we joined with the ARVN (Army of the Republic of Vietnam) Airborne Division in air assaults and overland attacks north of Bong Son. The ARVN was on the east along the coast, and we operated west of Route 1.

In these attacks we were successful in spite of bad weather in finding, fixing, and destroying enemy units as large as battalions who were defending strongly fortified positions. Our engineers also built a fine airstrip at position 'Dog' in 2½ days. When enemy troops saw that they could not hold the fortified areas, they began to break up into very small groups and to retreat to the north and to the west.

We then turned our attention to the high ground lying between the coastal plain and the An Lao Valley and to the An Lao Valley itself.

The next play involved a combined operation with the U.S. Marines blocking escape routes out of the valley.

Our attack into the An Lao Valley met only light resistance, and we killed or drove out the enemy that was present in a few days. About 4,500 out of a total population of around 8,000 inhabitants (of the An Lao Valley) did elect to leave their homes in the valley and move to an area under government control. We flew more than 3,300 of these people to freedom in our aircraft.

While the 2nd Brigade was thus engaged, our 3rd Brigade made an air assault into an enemy base area at which we had long wanted a crack. This was the area we had dubbed the "Eagle Claw" or "Crow's Foot."

The 2nd Brigade then air assaulted position "Pete" and the "Iron Triangle." (The "Iron Triangle" was named for its shape by cavalrymen during Masher/White Wing and was not the often-mentioned area near Saigon some 235 miles away.)

In this fight, the 2nd Brigade employed all their organic weapons plus much supporting artillery, tactical air support, tear gas, and a B-52 strike.

These actions of the 2nd Brigade accounted for many enemies killed, wounded, and captured, plus many large weapons captured or destroyed. In addition, there is much evidence that the enemy installations did include a VC regimental headquarters.

The final phase of White Wing, called Black Horse, was aimed at destroying whatever hostile forces were in the Cay Giep mountain stronghold.

The assault was made by bombing holes in the woods that cover most of the mountain and then by rappelling and by the use of our Chinook ladders to get onto the dominant high ground to sweep down the hills. No large numbers of VC were killed, but many were captured

Troops waiting for a ride to the next fight

Calling in airstrikes on NVA positions

and the myth of this being a strong enemy base was exploded.

So on March 6, our operations ended with our forces back in the area south of Bong Son where we had started 41 days before. We had made a 360-degree traverse around Bong Son in which for 41 consecutive days we had been in contact with the enemy.

In those 41 days we had done these things:

With the ARVN, we had made possible to:

A. Return 140,000 Vietnamese to GVN (Government of Vietnam) control through clearing the enemy from the coastal plain north of Bong Son.

B. We gave the inhabitants of An Lao and Son Long Valleys a chance to be freed of VC domination by moving to areas that are under GVN control.

C. We struck a very hard blow at enemy units that had long threatened Bong Son and Route 1 from Qui Nhon to Bong Son.

Air Cav artillery inflicted heavy casualties on enemy forces

Totals for Operation Masher/ White Wing

During the operation, 1,342 enemy were killed by body count; 593 were captured, including a battalion commander, a mortar company commander, and the executive officer of a regimental headquarters company; 1,060 enemy suspects were detained; 483 Viet Cong defected; 203 individual weapons were captured; and 52 crew-served weapons were taken, including one 105mm howitzer, ten 12.7mm and three .50 cal. anti-aircraft machine guns.

In short, Sky Troopers of the 1st Air Cav, you have placed the name and the fighting reputation of the 'First Team' at the very top of the roll of Army divisions. You have again given the Army and our country cause to be proud of you. Well done; I salute you.

Captured Communist flag with enemy weapons

After a bath and a chance to give their weapons a good cleaning, First

Air Cavalry assaults kept the NVA off balance

Team elements were again on their way, this time to an old stomping ground, Suoi Ca, or Happy Valley.

They encountered little enemy resistance here during the operation dubbed, 'Jim Bowie,' but according to cavalry officials, again made it clear to the Viet Cong that the valley would remain out of their hands.

Rich, fertile Happy Valley, fully under Viet Cong control a year ago, was the scene of the first major cavalry operation in Vietnam and now is one of the most successful pacification projects conducted by U.S. forces thus far in Vietnam.

While searching the hills surrounding the valley, Cavalry troops captured large quantities of enemy equipment.

As 'Jim Bowie' ended, Operation Lincoln, on the plateau between Pleiku and the Cambodian border kicked off. Elements of the division's 1st Brigade swept the Chu Pong hill mass and Ia Drang Valley, scene of heavy fighting between Cavalrymen and North Vietnamese regulars last November.

Contact for the overall operation was light, but cavalrymen reported several sharp clashes near the Cambodian border.

During Lincoln and its second phase called 'Mosby,' cavalry forces reported killing 450 Viet Cong and North Vietnamese regulars. First Team elements also captured 17 enemy.

By the operation's end, the Viet Cong had lost some 93 individual and 8 crew-served weapons to the Sky Troopers as well as 19,000 lbs. of rice."

The 227 Assault Helicopter Battalion provided
transport and gun ships

Captured Weapons from Operation Masher/White Wing

The enemy lost weapons of every size and caliber

Captured Communist anti-aircraft guns

Rockets of every caliber were captured

Captured 9 mm French sub machine guns

The enemy lost hundreds of rifles

Grenades of every type were captured

Russian SKS-45, Chicom AK-47, 9 mm Swedish model k

Russian SKS-45, Russian/Chicom AK-47

Soviet RPD and Chicom 56 light machine gun

Soviet SGMB and Chicom 57

57 mm recoilless rifle (Chicom type 36)

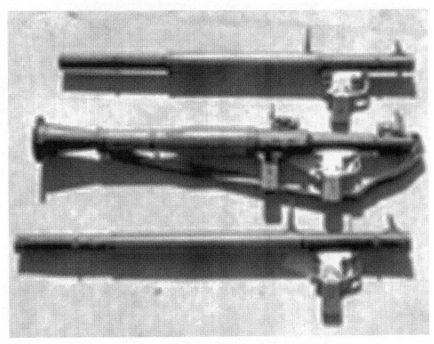

Soviet-produced RPG 2, RPG 7

VI
Eagle Flight to
Landing Zone Hereford

Special Forces-led CIDG troops are briefed on tactics

It began almost by accident. It was early May 1966 when patrols of the South Vietnamese Civilian Irregular Defense Groups (CIDG), led by American Special Forces advisors, found themselves encountering unusually large enemy formations flooding into their area of operations in the Vinh Thanh Valley. Enemy documents captured by the American-led CIDG indicated that several main-force NVA units were converging in the valley for a possible attack on the local Special Forces Camp. The enemy forces gathering in the valley were apparently survivors of units that had been badly mauled by the 1st Air Cav's recent Operation Masher/White Wing.

The NVA's plan was to marshal their forces, lick their wounds, and attack the lightly defended Special Forces Camp, which they figured would be easy pickings. A quick victory would be a good morale booster for the enemy soldiers who had been suffering defeat after defeat in their recent encounters with the troopers of the 1st Air Cav. The captured enemy documents provided a windfall to the top brass of the 1st Air Cavalry. Armed with accurate knowledge of enemy unit locations and dispositions, it appeared to be a great opportunity to flex some airmobile muscle. The paratroopers of the 1st (All the Way) Brigade led the attack into the valley.

The first unit to assault into the area was B Company, 2nd Battalion (Airborne), 8th Cavalry, commanded by Captain J.D. Coleman. Upon landing, the soldiers immediately made contact with a large enemy force, primarily the 18th Viet Cong Main Force Regiment. Although surrounded and outnumbered, the paratroopers fought the enemy to a bloody standstill. This was to be the first of many vicious battles and cruel ambushes that rolled back and forth across the Vinh Thanh Valley for 21 grueling days. During the operation the troopers of the Air Cav killed more than 500 enemy soldiers and wounded several times that number. Upon conclusion of what would be known as "Operation Crazy Horse," the newly appointed Division Commander of the 1st Air Cavalry, Major General John Norton, remarked, "Operation Crazy Horse was started by mistake....the enemy's, not ours."

*Major General
John Norton*

Return to Base Camp

After a brutal month of combat in the Central Highlands of Binh Dinh Province, the paratroopers of A Company, 2nd Battalion (Airborne), 8th Cavalry, returned to the 1st Cavalry Division base camp at An Khe on March 5, 1966. For the soldiers of A Company, this respite offered an opportunity to rest without having to be constantly vigilant, to clean and replace equipment, to eat something other than c-rations, and to remember our comrades who did not return with us.

It was during this time that Specialist Garry Bowles, the senior company aid man, requested transfer to a rifle platoon. Having been trained as an infantryman prior to attending combat medic school, his request was granted, and he was assigned to Lieutenant Gill Cochran's 2nd Platoon as an M-60 machine gunner. After a couple of weeks of "humping the hog," he was promoted to buck sergeant and eventually given leadership of the 2nd Platoon's pony recon team, a five-man team whose job it was to drop into the jungle and conduct reconnaissance patrols. During February, troopers operated east of the An Khe base camp, crushing some North Vietnamese units attempting to penetrate toward the coastal cities along the South China Sea. After a short break, they turned their attention to the west, toward the Cambodian border. Throughout the war, the North Vietnamese Army came south along the Ho Chi Minh trail, turning east at various strategic locations to attack into South Vietnam. One of these locations was in the Chu Pong Mountain, Ia Drang Valley area where the 1st Cav had fought the first major battles of the war the previous fall.

Journeying West

Although the 1st Cav was the most mobile combat unit in the history of warfare, with more than 400 helicopters at its disposal, as well as parachute capability, its movement west was by 2½-ton truck. Troopers left the An Khe base camp and traveled along Highway 19, the strategic route through the Central Highlands running from Pleiku in the west to Qui Nhon on the South China Sea. Not every-

Alpha Raiders cross over into Cambodia

Sid Shearing along the
Cambodian border

one realized the great historical significance to the journey west. On June 6, 1954, the French Mobile Group 100 had followed this exact route and was ambushed and destroyed by overwhelming Viet Minh forces, resulting in a devastating defeat for France. As troopers crossed through the Mang Yang Pass, Lieutenant Marty Stango, 1st Platoon leader, saw what he thought were hundreds of manhole covers dotting the terrain. He soon realized these were cylinders holding the remains of the French soldiers killed 12 years before by elements of the Viet Minh 803rd Regiment. The actual ambush occurred approximately 15 kilometers west of the village at An Khe.

Some wondered why the troops had not flown west in helicopters. Grunts were not privy to the thinking of the division's senior commanders: they just did what they were told. Perhaps the thought was to throw a direct challenge at the North Vietnamese infantry who undoubtedly lurked in the towering hills of the Mang Yang Pass as we drove through. We were frequently used as bait in the attempts to lure the NVA out for a fight. In any event, the enemy chose not to disrupt our journey. Perhaps the helicopter gun ships, aerial rocket artillery orbiting overhead, and the big guns of the 1st Cavalry artillery support from An Khe had something to do with the safe passage.

Along the Cambodian Border

We arrived without incident in the vicinity of Pleiku, the westernmost major city in the Central Highlands of Vietnam, the first mission was to establish a forward operating base, called LZ Oasis. This would become one of the largest American bases in the area and home to the 4th Infantry Division that would soon reinforce the 1st Cavalry Division.

"One of the strategic tragedies of the war," recalls Lieutenant Ed Polonitza, "was our inability to fight the enemy close to or in

Cambodia. There was no reason for this other than we were forbidden to do so by Pentagon edict. As a result, every time we pounded the North Vietnamese, they would scurry across the Cambodian border to lick their wounds. On this occasion, however, for some unknown reason,

Arriving at LZ Oasis

we were ordered to conduct combat operations along the Cambodian border. Our mission was to set up defensive positions and dig in. Again, we were put out as bait in an attempt to entice the North Vietnamese located to the west of us. Our defensive positions were established on a ridgeline that marked the border between the two countries.

One of the realities of the war in Vietnam was that only very rarely was an officer above the rank of captain actually on the ground in a combat situation. As a result, the lieutenants and captains leading the rifle platoons and companies engaged with the enemy made crucial tactical and sometimes strategic decisions. Doing what was right in order to accomplish the mission, as well as protecting the soldiers whose lives were entrusted to me, always drove my decisions. I am sure most of my fellow junior officers felt the same way.

Sometimes, however, these priorities could conflict with the Pentagon-imposed rules. So we did what we felt was right and didn't ask. Sitting astride the Cambodian border created a difficult dilemma. We could passively wait for the NVA to attack without notice, or we could create a more tactically sound situation by placing observation and listening posts forward of our positions, while running small reconnaissance patrols to the west. These latter options would result in penetrating the Cambodian border. We could request permission from higher headquarters to do this and probably be denied, or we could just do it. Needless to say, Alpha Company soldiers did spend some time over the Cambodian border during our operations in the western provinces. Extensive patrolling, numerous combat assaults, and many minor skirmishes filled each day during the months of March and April. From the standpoint of the combat infantrymen of Alpha Company, it was all fairly routine. But the month of May 1966 would be anything but routine, as we would once again be part of one of the most significant combat operations of the Vietnam War, Operation Crazy Horse.

Operation Crazy Horse

East of our base at An Khe lay a series of ridgelines and valleys running from north to south. At the foot of these ridgelines and valleys was Highway 19, the main route through the Central Highlands. During the war these valleys were a main infiltration route for the North Vietnamese Army. The Vinh Thanh Valley was the scene of many fierce battles between the NVA and the Sky Troopers of the 1st Cavalry Division. In an ironic twist, Vinh Thanh Valley was nicknamed, Happy Valley. Operation Crazy Horse began on May 16, 1966. Patrols from the Special Forces camp in Vinh Thanh discovered enemy documents and equipment indicating a major attack on the camp was imminent. The 1st Brigade of the 1st Cavalry Division airlifted into the valley with orders to destroy the enemy forces in the vicinity of Happy Valley.

A Company deployed into the valley, and my 3rd Platoon, temporarily attached to Delta Company, was assigned the mission of ambushing along the jungle trails leading from the northern end of the valley into the ridgelines above. We moved out on foot from the battalion command post located at the Special Forces Camp in the valley floor. Shortly before

Jungle listening post

dusk, we found an ambush site. It was a small clearing along a recently used trail. Our plan was to establish an L-shaped ambush so that we could hit an enemy unit from both the flank and front. We established listening posts several hundred meters each way down the trail. The job of the listening post was to give us early warning of approaching enemy. Although only a small unit, my platoon had more than adequate firepower to take on almost anything that would be moving down that trail. All of our riflemen were armed with M-16 rifles capable of fully automatic fire. We had two M-60 machine guns, which could deliver thousands of rounds into an enemy formation. Each of our three rifle squads had two grenadiers armed with M-79 grenade launchers capable of firing high explosive rounds up to 400 meters. We had hand grenades and claymore mines, electrically detonated and loaded with hundreds of metal pellets that could rip through an enemy formation with devastating results.

As darkness approached, Platoon Sergeant James C. Lester and I were doing a final check of our positions. We stood at the edge of the jungle looking into the clearing to ensure our firing positions had complete coverage of the ambush site. As our listening posts prepared to move into place, we suddenly heard loud laughter and saw beams of light

3rd Platoon command post

from the far end of our ambush. My first thought was that some of our guys were having a moment of insanity and had forgotten where they were. But then we saw two NVA soldiers walking right through our ambush site, flashlights on, talking loudly, and laughing at their own jokes. They passed no more than 10 meters from where Sergeant Lester and I were standing and obviously had no idea they were walking through 35 heavily armed paratroopers waiting to kill them. These were undoubtedly the luckiest soldiers in Vietnam at that moment, as Sergeant Lester and I decided to let them pass with the hope of a bigger target later that night.

The night passed quietly. But just before dawn, our left flank listening post reported movement coming toward it. Specialist Jim Rockwell, who was manning this LP, reported two enemy soldiers passing his position. When they entered the clearing, all hell broke loose. Our L-shaped ambush exploded with automatic fire from our machine guns and M-16s.

One of the North Vietnamese soldiers was killed instantly and the other severely wounded. None of us knew whether these were the same two who had walked through our ambush the night before, but, whoever they were, their luck had run out. Having compromised our position with the roar of gunfire, we quickly regrouped and moved back through the jungle, closing on the battalion command post later that morning.

One issue we had to deal with prior to closing out our ambush site was the wounded NVA soldier. Even though he was in bad shape, he could be a valuable intelligence resource. Additionally, the two enemy casualties had a number of documents that could also be critical. In order to expedite this situation, Specialist Mike Friedrichs and three others constructed a makeshift litter and hauled the wounded enemy to another friendly unit operating nearby. In turn, the unit would take the prisoner to a helicopter landing zone for extraction to an interrogation area. Mike and his small group then rejoined us at a predetermined check point for the movement back to the battalion CP.

My platoon, along with the rest of A Company, was then assigned as battalion Eagle Flight and security for the command post. Our sister units were conducting search and destroy missions in the mountains above us, and, in many cases, fighting pitched battles with the North Vietnamese infantrymen swarming the hills. The battalion Eagle Flight mission required that we be a quick reaction force to reinforce any friendly units that might need help in overcoming enemy resistance. Supporting our

Eagle flight to Hereford

Eagle Flight mission were six UH1 troop-carrying helicopters we called 'slicks,' several helicopter gun ships, and an artillery battery co-located with the battalion CP.

The morning of May 21 started routinely enough. Father Rogers, the battalion chaplain, was saying Mass at the battalion command post area. The skies were overcast, and a light rain fell. To the east and above us, Charlie Company, 1st Battalion, 12th Cavalry, began a search and destroy mission from LZ Hereford, where it had been located the previous night. LZ Hereford was a small helicopter landing zone located in what we called a saddle, which is a terrain feature characterized by a lower area flanked by two hills. LZ Hereford was located right in the saddle. By definition, this is an extremely precarious tactical area, since an enemy force manning the high

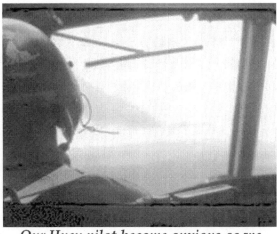

Our Huey pilot became anxious as we approached Hereford

ground would have a significant advantage over troops located in the saddle. Upon leaving Hereford, Charlie Company proceeded down the ridgelines toward the valley floor, searching for NVA reported in that area. Charlie Company's mortar platoon stayed at LZ Hereford to provide fire support to the advancing rifle platoons. From our position in the valley floor, we could hear the thump of Charlie Company's mortars supporting the advance. Later that morning, clouds and fog began to roll in, blocking our view of the mountaintops. Around noon, the quiet in the valley was broken by the sound of automatic weapons fire echoing between the hills. Frantic radio traffic told us that the mortar platoon on LZ Hereford was being attacked by an overwhelming enemy force firing down from the two hills above the saddle, as well as by NVA infantry charging in the tall grass around the LZ.

Our company was immediately ordered to load up on the six Eagle Flight slicks sitting at the battalion CP and assault into LZ Hereford to reinforce the beleaguered mortar platoon. My 3rd Platoon was to be the lead element of A Company into the LZ. As each Huey could hold six infantrymen, my platoon would have the first lift of the six choppers.

We quickly loaded up, realizing we would be going into a hot LZ surrounded on two sides by high ground swarming with NVA machine gunners. I loaded into the first helicopter, along with Staff Sergeant Isaac Guest and his rifle squad. The helicopter engines were roaring, the main rotor rotating fiercely. The pilot pointed toward the LZ that was now completely covered with fog. This poor visibility made it impossible to land on the LZ. Despite the noise from the helicopter engines, we could hear the sounds of gunfire from Hereford. We sat on the choppers waiting for a break in the fog. Finally, the low-hanging clouds parted briefly and we were in the air for the short flight to the LZ. Halfway up, the clouds closed again, and our pilots had to turn back. Almost as soon as we approached the battalion area, the clouds parted once again. We turned back toward LZ Hereford.

Specialist Mike Friedrichs had recently rejoined 3rd Platoon after being seriously wounded during a February firefight. Sitting on the floor of the troop compartment of his slick, Mike recognized the pilot, a Hispanic major who had flown us on a number of previous combat assaults. From past experience, Mike learned to get a read on his level of anxiety by watching the veins on his neck. During this short flight, the pilot's veins were bulging. 'I knew we were in for something big,' thought Mike as his chopper charged toward LZ Hereford.

Lieutenant Polonitza recalls, "As we approached the LZ, I was on one landing strut of the helicopter, and Specialist Leonard Lawrence was on the other one. Hereford was a small LZ, so only one Huey at a time could land. We had to get out of the choppers fast so others could bring in the rest of our company as quickly as possible.

I leaped into the LZ along with Specialist Lawrence. He landed on top of a dead American soldier, his M16 barrel twisted at a grotesque angle. Each helicopter followed in quick succession. Specialist Jim Rockwell rode in on the second Huey. He jumped into the mortar pit where three dead cavalrymen had been killed while attempting to bring fire against the attackers. Specialist Juan Fernandez was the youngest soldier in the 3rd Platoon, having celebrated his 18th birthday a few days before arriving in Vietnam the previous August. As he scrambled out of his slick and into the LZ, all he could see were bodies lying everywhere. We quickly set up a hasty perimeter around the LZ, but it was obvious we were too late. The enemy had fled moments before leaving behind the bodies of 19 dead American soldiers.

The remaining rifle platoons of A Company arrived at LZ Hereford just behind us. At almost the same time, the remainder of C Company, which had reversed itself and scrambled back to the LZ in a frantic attempt to help its mortar platoon, approached the saddle area. Soon, four mortar platoon soldiers, all wounded, struggled back into our security perimeter. They had slipped down the side of the ridgeline to escape the enemy onslaught. Captain Forman, our company commander quickly established control of the LZ. He told me to police up all the equipment we could from the dead and wounded. He calmly said, 'They won't be needing it anymore.' Among the items we found on the LZ were a number of crude North Vietnamese propaganda leaflets, primarily targeted at our black soldiers, making references to the 'Ku Klux Klan back home.' Other than as an interesting curiosity, these had no effect.

As soon as the LZ was secured, we were ordered to pursue the enemy force that had attacked the mortar platoon. We moved west across the heavily jungled ridgeline, where we felt the NVA had retreated. As we advanced, we saw that our artillery fire had been effective in pounding the fleeing enemy. Our trail was littered with dead bodies. One appeared to be much larger and in a different uniform than the typical Vietnamese infantryman. We thought he might have been a Chinese advisor to the North Vietnamese. If so, his advisory duties had been terminated, compliments of the 1st Cav artillery.

As night approached, Captain Forman directed us to pull into a tight defensive perimeter on a ridge top overlooking the Vinh Thanh valley. We felt the enemy's presence as we dug in for the night. As night fell, a torrential rain began. The night was impossibly black with the heavy rain and cloud cover. My radio operator, Specialist Gary Mierzejewski, Platoon Sergeant Lester, and myself were clustered a short distance behind our security perimeter. Around midnight, we heard peculiar tapping noises above the sound of the falling rain. At first, we didn't realize

RTO Gary Mierzejewski

what this noise was. Then a small rock hit a tree not far from our position. We then knew we had NVA scouts crawling toward our position trying to draw fire to pinpoint our automatic weapons. Once they knew our strong points, they would attack around our machine guns and attempt to overrun our perimeter.

Sergeant Lester and I had very little control over the situation at that point. We had only voice communications with our perimeter security, and to attempt to move forward in the blinding rain would be impossible.

We had to trust in the discipline and alertness of our forward positions. Our trust was well placed. Specialist Ansel Boyce manned a security position a few meters in front of us. A machine gunner, Boyce was also armed with a 45-caliber pistol. As we waited tensely, a single shot exploded from Boyce's pistol, followed immediately by the low moan of a dying North Vietnamese scout. Soon, a second shot fired by another machine gunner everybody called 'Smitty,' killed another scout. As we waited through that endless, miserable night, the actions of these two brave troopers discouraged the NVA lurking around our perimeter from another attempt against us.

As dawn broke, Sergeant Garry Bowles examined the bodies of the two dead enemy soldiers, who had fallen virtually on top of our perimeter. One had six pairs of what we called 'Ho Chi Minh sandals' tied to his equipment. We felt these belonged to some of his other buddies probing barefoot around us during the night. After another few days of chasing the North Vietnamese out of Happy Valley, Operation Crazy Horse ended. Although Crazy Horse was very successful, with more than 500 enemy killed, the paratroopers of Alpha Company went back to An Khe with mixed emotions. Had the clouds parted a few minutes earlier on May 21, we may have been able to save the lives of at least some of the 19 Americans killed in action that day. To this day, Sergeant Louis Buckley, Jr., a member of the Charlie Company mortar platoon, remains missing in action. Perhaps if we had arrived a few minutes earlier, Sergeant Buckley could have been saved from whatever unknown fate had befallen him."

Elkins, Smitty, and Rockwell

VII
Death in a Small Place

NVA Assault

Virtually all of the 1st Cavalry infantry units that fought in Operation Crazy Horse were ferried into and out of the battle zone through a place called Landing Zone (LZ) Hereford. This was a small one- or two-ship LZ located in a saddle on a ridgeline overlooking Happy Valley. The rugged ridgelines to the east and west of the valley were dense jungle, and good landing zones were scarce. LZ Hereford, on the eastern side of the valley, was the only piece of open terrain leading into that enemy-infested sector of the Crazy Horse area of operations. Thus, this small piece of terrain took on great tactical importance to both sides. During the course of the operation, a goal of the 1st Cav was to keep this crucial LZ secure. The North Vietnamese constantly lurked in this area looking to ambush an American unit if they could achieve tactical surprise and superiority. Having been pounded by suppressing artillery and gunship fire every time a cavalry unit assaulted into Hereford, the LZ was a scarred, devastated wreck of a landscape.

On May 21, 1966, the mortar platoon of Charlie Company, 1st Battalion (Airborne), 12th Cavalry was located on LZ Hereford. Charlie Company had executed a combat assault into LZ Hereford several days before. After several days of "humping the boonies" as the cavalrymen described the search and destroy missions that made up their daily routine, Charlie Company returned to LZ Hereford. The company's three rifle platoons would begin a westward sweep from Hereford down to the valley floor looking for NVA infantrymen who might be in that area. The mortar platoon would stay at Hereford, fire its remaining rounds in support of the company's advance, and then would be extracted by helicopter to the battalion command post in the valley.

LZ Hereford was a tricky piece of terrain to defend. It was located on a saddle which is a military terrain feature characterized by a low-lying area surrounded on two sides by higher ground, in this case, two prominent hills. The key to defending a saddle is to secure the higher ground above the saddle. Otherwise, an enemy force could achieve significant tactical superiority by seizing the high ground, enabling devastating fire to be brought against the soldiers below. Unfortunately with only 22 cavalrymen, the mortar platoon did not have enough strength to man its mortars and simultaneously hold the high ground above Hereford. On May 21, this courageous but undermanned band would pay a severe price for its inability to secure these hills.

John Spranza manning
81 mm Mortar tube

Mortar Platoon Attacked

John Spranza is one of the few survivors of Charlie Company still alive to tell the tale of that horrific day. The mortar platoon was so few in number that it was unable to mount a traditional perimeter defense around the LZ. As many of the platoon's troopers were needed to fire their mortar, only a few soldiers were available to provide security. Sergeant Robert L. Kirby, the platoon leader, organized a u-shaped defense leaving a portion of the mortar platoon position completely undefended.

Specialist John Spranza radios for help

Around noon, Specialist John Spranza was talking on the platoon radio. He was communicating with the Charlie Company rifle platoons, helping adjust the mortar platoon's fire in support of the company's advance down the ridgeline toward the valley floor. Spranza recalls Charles Stuckey and Paul Harrison located in a nearby defensive position, suddenly opening fire with their M16s. "I thought they had gone crazy," Spranza remembers. "I couldn't immediately imagine what they were firing at or why." But just as Harrison and Stuckey opened fire, the LZ was raked by AK-47 rounds fired by hundreds of North Vietnamese infantrymen charging toward Hereford from the high ground above the landing zone. Interspersed with this automatic weapons fire was a barrage of rocket-propelled grenades arcing down toward the American positions.

Spranza rolled back into his foxhole and tried to reach for his radio that was the platoon's only communication with the rest of Charlie Company and any hope for reinforcement. Without help, the mortar platoon would be destroyed by the overwhelming firepower of the North Vietnamese human wave attack. "I had the long whip antenna on my radio and the gooks apparently saw it and were aiming RPGs right at me," recalls Spranza. He shot three North Vietnamese who were heading straight for his position but was wounded himself. "I was able to raise the company on the radio and told them we needed gun ships and artillery."

Realizing that its mortar platoon was under heavy attack, Charlie Company reversed its path and started moving as fast as possible back toward the LZ to help the beleaguered platoon. Unfortunately, the terrain, elephant grass, and "wait-a-minute" vines made movement very slow. At the same time, the battalion headquarters located in the valley below ordered A Company, 2nd Battalion (Airborne), 8th Cavalry, in reserve at the headquarters, to load on a section of Eagle Flight choppers and make an emergency combat assault into Hereford to rescue the mortar platoon. Once again the mortar platoon had no luck at all. As soon as the first lift of A Company boarded the Eagle Flight Hueys, a heavy fog rolled over Hereford making an immediate combat assault impossible.

The few remaining Americans who had not been killed in the initial North Vietnamese onslaught realized they were fighting for their lives and that the difficult terrain and the fog precluded any hope of assistance. Although seriously wounded, Specialist Spranza was able to crawl to a small rocky area that several survivors were using as a defensive position. Being unable to carry his radio with him, Spranza found a hand grenade and threw it back at the radio hoping to destroy it before the enemy could capture it.

NVA Troops charge across LZ Hereford

Thinking he would not survive much longer, he hid his classified radio codebook in his pants, hoping the North Vietnamese wouldn't look there if they searched his body. Sergeant Kirby, the platoon leader, had also made it to this improvised position, where these last few cavalrymen would make their final stand. Now out of ammunition, they grabbed for some AK-47s dropped by dead and wounded enemy. Kirby found several hand grenades that he threw at the North Vietnamese skirmishers now charging out of the elephant grass on the slopes of the LZ. When one NVA charged its position, Kirby shot him in the face with a flare pistol.

Journalist Killed

Joining the mortar platoon that morning arriving on a resupply helicopter was 31-year-old Sam Castan, a journalist for *Look* magazine. He was working on an article for *Look* but was having trouble finding a combat situation to photograph. Every time he went to a battle site, the fighting stopped. He referred to himself as the luckiest guy in Vietnam. But that day, his luck would run out. After surviving the initial North Vietnamese fire, he tried to escape by running down the side of the ridgeline to safety. He ran right into an advancing group of enemy where he was shot in the head and killed.

Eagle flight lands at LZ Hereford

Escaping to Safety

John Spranza, Kirby, and a few others also tried to crawl into the tall elephant grass to escape to safety. All of the survivors had been wounded, some several times. Specialist Spranza had been shot five times including taking one round in the head that knocked out most of his teeth. Sergeant Kirby had been shot three times. Both were bleeding badly and on the verge of unconsciousness. At this point, thinking that all the friendlies were dead, as there was no radio contact from the mortar platoon, artillery fire from the battery located in the valley floor began pounding the LZ. At the same time, the NVA infantrymen were searching for any remaining Americans in the tall elephant grass and shooting any wounded.

Sergeant Kirby, knowing that the few remaining cavalrymen were out of ammunition and bleeding from numerous wounds, felt that their chances of survival would be better back on the LZ. He thought the NVA would have pulled out from the LZ due to the pounding of the American artillery. Spranza told Kirby to save himself if he could. Spranza was so shot up that he could no longer move. His only hope of survival was to lie down and

Field hospital at Camp Radcliff

play dead and hope the NVA was convinced of his demise. Several times, enemy soldiers rolled him over and searched his pockets but each time moved on thinking he was dead. Spranza lay as still as he could feeling that he would bleed to death in the tall elephant grass. At this point, several 1st Cav gun ships flew by, strafing the LZ in preparation for A Company's combat assault into Hereford. One fired its machine guns so close to Spranza that dirt kicked up by the impacting rounds hit him in the face.

On the verge of unconsciousness, Specialist Spranza had hidden his bayonet under his body and decided he would kill the next North Vietnamese who searched him. Feeling hands probing his body, he turned and reached out with his bayonet. He looked up into the face of a Charlie Company soldier just arriving back at the LZ. The enemy had fled and choppers bringing A Company into Hereford began to land. Specialist John Spranza had survived this horrific attack but lapsed into unconsciousness. He next remembered being on a surgery table at the field hospital at the 1st Cavalry base camp at An Khe.

The Price They Paid

Over the coming months, Spranza would be evacuated through a series of military hospitals finally winding up at Womack Army Hospital in Fort Bragg, North Carolina. Of the 23 Americans who were on LZ Hereford on that fateful day of May 21, 1966, only four survived: John Spranza, Sergeant Kirby, and Specialists Isaac Johnson and Charles Stuckey. One member of the platoon, Sergeant Louis Buckley is still missing in action. Spranza recalls Sergeant Buckley, wounded in the shoulder, running across the LZ to his fighting position but never saw him again.

Although the North Vietnamese may have succeeded in overrunning and virtually destroying Charlie Company's mortar platoon, they too paid a terrible price for their success. More than 60 dead NVA infantrymen littered the LZ and the area surrounding it. While they were vastly outnumbered and outgunned, the cavalrymen on LZ Hereford were not outfought. Every American soldier who died on that forsaken hill fought to the end and made a timeless contribution to the heroic tradition of the 1st Cavalry Division.

Charlie Company Mortars KIAs
May 21, 1966

BENJAMIN ROBERT LEE, PFC
BENTON HENRY, PFC
BRAME CLARENCE RAY, PFC
BROOKS JAMES FRANCIS JR., PFC
BUCKLEY, LOUIS, SGT
CROCKER DAVID STEPHEN, SP4
DRUMMOND AUSTIN LEON, SP4
GAINES CHARLES A., SGT
HARRISON PAUL JAMES, SP4
MACK HAROLD JR., PFC
POST DANIEL GIBSON, SP4
SHEPHERD EDWARD, PSGT
SPIKES A.V., SP4
TAMAYO JOEL, PFC
TASTE WADE, PFC
WILLIAMS LONNIE CLIFFORD, PFC

VIII
Changing of the Guard
Pony Soldier Summer

Returning home after 365 days

During the early summer of 1966, big changes were taking place in A Company, 2nd Battalion (Airborne), 8th Cavalry. The paratroopers who had arrived by troop transport the previous year were going home, their 365-day tour of duty completed. Gone were the experienced platoon leaders, platoon sergeants, and the ordinary troopers who had lived and fought together for 12 months. During the previous year the paratroopers of A Company had developed into a tough, cohesive combat unit. With their departure, the Alpha Raiders became a shell of their former selves. What remained were about 50 combat veterans including officers, NCOs, and infantrymen, most of whom had arrived in country after November 1965. New faces were arriving daily from the States. More than 100 replacements arrived that summer to fill the numerous vacant slots in the company roster. These included new riflemen, NCOs, platoon leaders, and a new company commander, Captain David Bouton, who took command in late June, the company's fourth captain in a year. That summer the battalion also got its third new battalion commander in 12 months, Lieutenant Colonel Thomas Tackaberry. To the dismay of the handful of remaining "old timers," the vast majority of the replacements weren't paratroopers. In fact, most of the new troopers were fresh out of infantry training and had been in the Army for fewer than 20 weeks.

The old timers also watched as the sign over the company street at the An Khe Base camp was replaced. Down came "Airborne Alpha Raiders" and up went a sign proclaiming that we were now "Bouton's Batmobile Batmen." The new "nom de guerre" was less than inspiring to the old timers, but the new guys loved it. It gave them a much-needed sense of unit cohesion and became who they were. It was obvious that A Company was becoming less airborne and more airmobile. Captain Bouton proved to be an excellent combat leader, and the new guys learned fast. The 3rd Platoon Leader, Lieutenant Ed Polonitza, was promoted to Company Executive Officer and worked with Captain Bouton to bring A Company back to its previous level of combat effectiveness.

Due to some glitch in paperwork, Specialist Leonard Lawrence,

Bouton's Batmobile Batmen

the venerable 3rd Platoon point man, did not receive orders to rotate home that summer with his buddies. Someone had goofed, and Leonard had to hunker down and soldier on.

Late in the spring of 1966, Battalion Headquarters initiated a program called "fragmentation." The program cannibalized various platoons in the battalion and created "pony teams," five-man teams whose mission was to drop into the jungle and perform extended reconnaissance patrols. The pony team had been around in one form or another since the battalion had first taken the field in October 1965. Alpha Company had been one of the first companies in the battalion to develop effective pony teams.

Pony team rescue

"I remember my first exposure to a pony team," recalls Sergeant Garry Bowles. "It was the previous winter, and we were on operations along the Cambodian border. I remember it was very cold and wet. We had established an artillery firebase deep in the jungle and had been beating the bush for several days. One morning, right after breakfast, a lot of excited traffic started to erupt on all A Company radios at the firebase. It seems a pony team had run into a full company of NVA infantry literally marching down a trail. The team was spotted by the NVA and, after firing a full magazine per man into the massed enemy formation, the team fled back down the trail to a pre-arranged LZ for extraction. I stood in the middle of the firebase; I could hear the distant whomp, whomp, whomp of an approaching Huey. I watched as the chopper appeared over the tree line; it was moving very slowly. As it cleared the jungle canopy, I understood the reason for its cautious approach. Hanging from the Huey was 100 feet of rope, and on that rope was a five-man pony team, each man hanging on for dear life. As they landed, I and others ran forward to their aid.

The team Lieutenant, Bill Marr, was helping his men to their feet as we arrived. I remember that they were all soaking wet and shivering like mad. I recall the team's point man, Gary Sculac, his teeth chattering as he talked a mile a minute, explaining how he rounded a bend in the trail and saw the entire North Vietnamese Army standing in front of him. I remember thinking, 'What a gutsy bunch of guys.'"

A pony team consisted of a team leader, generally a buck sergeant, an RTO, a point man, and two automatic weapons men. The mission of the pony team was to find the enemy soldiers and accurately plot their position so rifle platoons, airpower, or artillery could destroy them. "I called it sneaking and peeping," recalls Sergeant Bowles. The pony team's job was to find the enemy, not to fight the enemy, but many times contact was unavoidable. During the summer of 1966, the 2nd Battalion (Airborne) of the 8th Cavalry fielded 10 pony teams. More than half of the battalion's pony teams that summer came from the A Company weapons platoon and second rifle platoon.

Operation Nathan Hale

The last week of June 1966, Captain Bouton joined A Company as its new commanding officer. Captain Bouton was a Notre Dame graduate, and, until taking over A Company, had served as division commander Major General Kinnard's aide. Most combat infantrymen are suspicious of change when it comes to company commanders. This new leader was

C-130 transport to Tuy Hoa

somebody everyone in A Company was curious about. He certainly had what was called "command presence." His build was solid, with ramrod military posture, his face determined, his voice clear, and his language direct. He had a remarkable memory, and within a few days, was calling everyone by name and rank. He demonstrated an outward confidence that certainly gave everyone in the ranks some much-needed reassurance.

He also carried a very distinctive weapon that made him stand out from the crowd. It was an experimental model of the AR-15, a little snub nose version of the M-16 that everyone else carried. In addition to looking short and mean, it had some nifty features, including a collapsible stock and the ability to fire in a "burst" of three to four rounds with one pull of the trigger. The grunts all admired the weapon and looked forward to hearing it fired on "burst." The rumor was that Captain Bouton was given the weapon by a delegation from Colt manufacturing on a visit to General Kinnard.

Captain Bouton's assignment to the Alpha Raiders was no random transfer. Alpha Company Commander Captain James Detrixhe, who was killed four months earlier on February 24, was a good friend of Bouton's. They had served together as aides at division headquarters, and Bouton had requested the transfer to A Company. The fact that he was hunting for some payback for his friend's death was a good thing to the troopers who had fought under Captain Detrixhe earlier that year.

Shortly after Captain Bouton arrived, the entire company boarded C-130 aircraft and flew to Tuy Hoa on the coast of South Vietnam. On June 26, the troopers climbed aboard Huey choppers and made their first air assault of what was to become known as Operation Nathan Hale. The company secured an LZ designated, "Quarter," and immedi-ately commenced pony team patrols, setting up

Operation Nathan Hale meant more air assaults for the Alpha Raiders

several night ambush positions. The only report of enemy activity that night was from a pony recon team commanded by Sergeant Jack "Snake" Fortenberry, indicating enemy forces were moving north of his position. No contact with the enemy unit was made. The next day, Captain Bouton deployed Lieutenant Ed Polonitza's 3rd Platoon into a valley northwest of the company's location to find and destroy enemy gun positions that had been firing on Air Cav helicopters in the area. No enemy positions were located.

Later that day Sergeant Fortenberry hit pay dirt. As Alex "Pony" Dziekonski recalls, "We were moving in our usual line of march. Strong was on point, Jerry was right behind him, then came Fortenberry, then me, with Osh Kosh bringing up the rear. Our mission was to scout along a major enemy supply route, hoping to find any large enemy formations. We located a small enemy village that appeared to be a supply point and manned by at least an NVA platoon. We radioed our contact, Hard Anvil Six/Five at battalion headquarters and were informed that Delta Company would soon be moving into the location we had just targeted. Hard Anvil Six/Five congratulated us for a job well done and ordered us back on our mission. As we quietly melted back into the jungle to resume our long-range recon patrol, we passed Delta troops as they moved into position to assault the NVA encampment we had just found. Within minutes, machine gun fire,

Patrolling down jungle stream

automatic weapons fire, and M-79 grenade explosions could be heard coming from the enemy camp. We pushed further into the jungle, monitoring all radio traffic as we moved. All reports indicated Delta caught the NVA completely by surprise and killed or captured them all without losing a man.

The next morning we were ordered to hook up with A Company. We arrived at the A Company location around noon. The company had been working all morning, clearing an LZ that could handle enough helicopters to extract the entire company to a new operational area.

Shortly after the LZ was completed, the new battalion commander, Lieutenant Colonel Tackaberry, arrived in his tactical operations center chopper to brief us on our new mission. The Colonel stood on a small knoll, declared the area to be free of NVA, and informed us we would be extracted from this location and air assaulted into a new area of operations in order to find the enemy. He then strode back to his chopper and left the LZ. As the Colonel's chopper cleared the tree line at the far edge of the landing zone, it was taken under intense enemy automatic weapons fire, as were all subsequent choppers in the extraction. June 27 found A Company operating from LZ Knife, again running patrols all day and manning ambush sites all night. Several minor clashes with enemy forces resulted in several VC being killed and several captured. On July 2, Operation Nathan Hale ended with no A Company troopers killed during the campaign.

Operation Henry Clay

On July 3, the troopers of A Company found themselves once again engaged in air assault operations in a campaign named Henry Clay. To the men of A Company, it appeared to be merely an extension of Operation Nathan Hale from the previous month, as Specialist Jim Rockwell, a 3rd Platoon grenadier remarked, "Same game, different name." The rich fertile coastal plains around Tuy Hoa were familiar stomping grounds to the paratroopers of the "All The Way Brigade." They had been running operations in the area for more than a month.

On the second day, a platoon-sized operation led by Sergeant Duke DuShane discovered a battalion-sized enemy base camp. It was a newly constructed complex and well-concealed from aerial observation by a thick double jungle canopy. Orders were given to destroy the enemy base. Troopers placed explosive charges in what appeared to be a supply hooch and set fire to the remaining structures. The supply dump exploded with a roar, and the cached enemy ammunition erupted skyward in a crescendo of thousands of bursting bullets. Someone mentioned it was the 4th of July, and all 2nd Platoon troopers present agreed it was a great fireworks display. Over the next several weeks, A Company operated 24 hours a day, conducting patrols and manning ambush sites with no significant enemy contact.

On the night of July 21, a pony recon team lead by Sergeant Garry Bowles spotted two squads of enemy soldiers moving northwest of his position. The enemy unit was well-armed with both machine guns and mortars. The pony team radioed map coordinates of the enemy's location and line of march; both artillery and mortar fire were brought to bear on the enemy formation with good results. Sergeant Bowles reported three confirmed enemy killed and a lot of equipment destroyed. Numerous blood trails also led from the area, indicating that many of the fleeing survivors had been wounded.

Several days later, a pony team led by Sergeant Fortenberry was patrolling along a creek bed running around the base of a small mountain. As Alex Dziekonski recalls, "We were moving very slow and quiet along the edge of the creek bed when all of a sudden Strong, our point man, froze in place and raised his fist for our attention. Strong then walked down the trail, out of sight. Everyone stood there very still and very quiet,

Burning enemy encampment

our fingers on our triggers and our eyes slowly scanning the jungle around us. Automatic weapons fire suddenly opened up. The enemy soldiers' return fire was weak and erratic; they didn't know where we were exactly, and they were firing away from us toward our flank. Strong came running back up the trail hell bent for leather. 'Snake,' sensing this was a good time to exit the area, led the team in a rapid retreat up the mountain to high ground. Snake was yelling our coordinates to me and, in turn, I was feeding them into my radio handset as we scrambled up the mountain. As we crested the top of the mountain to a small clearing, lift ships arrived for a timely and grateful extraction to safety. Strong told us that when he halted us on the trail, he sensed something ahead of us. Going forward he came upon a stream where he found 6 to 10 NVAs, one of whom was very tall, possibly a Red Chinese advisor. Strong opened up on full automatic and was able to empty two full magazines into them before falling back. Hard Anvil Six/Five at Battalion Headquarters later told us we probably had bumped into an NVA command post of some sort, and the location was targeted for air strikes. A week later, Operation Henry Clay ended, and, as Specialist Jim Rockwell had remarked earlier that month, 'Same game, different name.'"

On October 8, 1966, Specialist Leonard Lawrence finally received his orders to return stateside; the orders had been lost since July. Having served 15 full months as the 3rd Platoon point man, Lawrence was at last returning home to his darling mother and beloved West Virginia.

Breaking In New Troops

October 15 initiated the "new guys" into the combat zone. Lieutenant Ed Polonitza recalls, "We were operating in Binh Dinh, at the foot of a series of ridge lines. I was XO and Captain Dave Bouton was CO. As morning broke, heavy fog settled over the area. We were notified that a chopper load of badly needed new replacements was arriving to help fill our manpower shortfall, but we couldn't get a chopper into our location because of the fog. We were gearing up for a search and destroy mission across the several ridge lines to our front. The CO needed to move out to get the mission accomplished, but he didn't believe there would be any LZs available in the heavily jungled ridge lines where the company would be operating. So, he told me to stay behind with an RTO, wait until the fog cleared, land the replacements, and then move around the base of the ridgelines to link up with the company that night as they completed the mission.

Around noon, the fog cleared, and we brought in the chopper with the new guys. We then started around the base of the ridge lines, making good time, since we were moving through fairly open terrain. The company had a rougher time, moving through heavy jungle and up and down the ridge lines. We reached the link up point late that afternoon, before the main body arrived, and discovered a North Vietnamese heavy machine gun position sitting at the edge of one of the ridges. I thought it was probably there to attack the Cav choppers that would be flying along the valley floor.

The machine gunner observed our approach and took us under fire. I'm sure this was a very interesting first day in the field for the replacements. We took cover, not wanting to expose the new guys at this point, and thought the best alternative was for me to take out the NVA gunners myself. While the rest of the group put down some covering fire, I crawled up the side of the ridge, put a grenade right in the middle of the machine gun crew, and took them all out. As night fell, we guided the company into our position with flares and successfully linked up with them. It was an interesting day."

Lieutenant Polonitza was awarded the Bronze Star Medal with "V" Device for heroism for his actions that day.

Sergeant Duke DuShane

Operation Thayer

As summer progressed into autumn, the men of A Company found themselves involved in yet another major action, this one named Operation Thayer. The pony teams that had been so successful the past summer were being dismantled. Alpha Company's rifle platoons needed all the men they could find for the upcoming campaign. The soldiers who had manned the pony teams were returned to their original platoons as squad leaders, RTOs, and point men. Sergeant Bowles and RTO

Dziekonski felt fortunate to be returned to the 2nd Platoon in the capable hands of Sergeant Duke DuShane, who at that time, due to the lack of lieutenants, was acting platoon leader. Sergeant Bowles, who had less than a month left in country, and Dziekonski, who had less than two months left on his tour of duty, both felt that the best way to survive, what little remained of their war, was to serve in a platoon led by the "Duke."

Pushing through the jungle

"We were a month and a half into Operation Thayer," recalls Lieutenant Ed Polonitza. "It was November 19, 1966. We were pushing hard through the jungle as we normally did on one of our many search and destroy missions. I was XO at the time and was in the rear part of our formation. I received a radio call from 'Batman,' which was Captain Bouton's call sign, ordering the column to halt and take up a defensive posture. The platoon leaders and myself were ordered forward to the CO's position. My first thought was that we had detected some enemy and were preparing for an assault. Captain Bouton told the platoon leaders and myself, that the AFN (Armed Forces Network) was carrying the Notre Dame-Michigan State football game, and we were going to pull into a perimeter while he listened to the game. At that point in the season, Notre Dame was undefeated and ranked #1 in the country; Michigan State was rated #2. So we listened to the game out there in the middle of the jungle. Bouton was quite disappointed as it ended in a 10-10 tie. It would have been bad luck for any NVA to have shown up during the game. The wrath Batman would have inflicted upon the hapless enemy would have been terrible indeed.

"The day after the 'big game,' we were extracted by choppers to a brigade-sized base camp down along the South China Sea," recalls Sergeant Bowles. "The name of the place was Tuy Hoa. We had been here before, passing through during various search and destroy missions. Its most distinguishing feature was a very impressive mountain that rose up from the flat coastal plain. It was also the home to an ever-expanding airstrip. After we off-loaded the Hueys, the company formed up, and we moved by platoons to our assigned sector of the defensive perimeter. As we marched from the airfield, I couldn't help but notice that there were artillery batteries dug in everywhere. I had never seen so much artillery at one firebase. There were not only a lot of Air Cav guns, but also artillery from the 101st Airborne and the South Korean Army.

We arrived at our sector of the line, all of us expecting to spend the morning digging in foxholes and constructing fighting positions. Much to our happy surprise, our section of the line came complete with foxholes and sandbagged positions already constructed and awaiting our arrival. These excellently con-structed fortifications were placed behind rows of razor wire and trip flares. We found out later that morning that this sector of the

Pony team extraction

perimeter was previously manned by a South Korean infantry outfit that had moved back to field on a patrol mission. It was a grunt's dream come true. It was almost like one of your buddies cleaning your weapon by mistake. All that work that we didn't have to do.

As we were settling into our new digs, Duke DuShane gave us the word that half of each squad could take a three-hour R and R on the beautiful stretch of beach we had seen when we choppered in earlier that morning. The Duke said two hours on the line and two hours on the beach would be the rotation, and he left it up to us squad leaders as to who was to go when. I hit the beach with the first group. The sand was white and clean, the sun warm, and the water was a beautiful crystal clear blue. It was like being on vacation. Up and down the beach, you could see troopers in their brown GI-issue boxer shorts. Some were sunbathing, others swimming or playing grab ass with their buddies, and some just sitting on the beach staring out at the horizon in solitary thought. It was wonderful!

That afternoon, around 1500 hours, we were told that Captain Bouton had arranged for the company to get a hot meal that night. The rumor was steak and chicken. It had been sever-

Tuy Hoa Mountain in the background

al weeks between hot meals and a couple of months in between steaks, so I was certainly looking forward to finding out what a steak tasted like again.

A couple of hours before chow, I was ordered to report to the company command post. I put on my helmet, grabbed my M-16, and headed to the CP. When I arrived, a staff sergeant asked me if I was Sergeant Bowles. 'Yes,' I answered.

'Your orders arrived a couple of days ago,' he replied, 'You're going stateside. You're going home!'

My toes and fingers began to tingle, and my stomach turned suddenly queasy. I knew I was a short-timer with less than a couple of weeks left on my tour, but I hadn't dwelled on the date, not wanting to jinx myself. Hearing the words 'You're going home' sort of knocked the wind out of me. I returned to my platoon's position along the line, not mentioning my good news to anyone. I figured I'd wait until the next morning to tell anyone, still wary of a jinx. The steak and chicken arrived as promised, and we all thoroughly enjoyed ourselves.

After chow, Captain Bouton further ingratiated himself with the troopers of A Company by announcing that there would be a company bonfire on the beach that night with lots of cold beer. As time progressed, this day just seemed to get better and better. My squad took the first watch on the perimeter that night; and we were relieved around 2100 hours so we could attend the bonfire and drink a couple of beers. A bunch of the new guys started singing the theme song to 'Batman,' the hit TV show back in the States, and since we were Bouton's Batmobile Batmen, the song seemed appropriate.

The next morning at first light I gathered my gear and started saying my goodbyes to all my buddies in A Company. There was just a handful of the old guard left: Jimmy Rockwell, Mike Friedrichs, Alex 'Pony' Dziekonski, Duke DuShane, Bobby Elkins, and Lieutenant Polonitza. These were the guys who were at my side as we fought across the rice paddies of Bong Son, up the steep mountains of the An Lao, and down the long jungle trails of the Cambodian border. As I made my way toward the airfield for the first leg of my return trip home, my feelings were confused. I should have been happier that I was going stateside. Instead I felt guilty that I was leaving my A Company buddies. I felt like I was leaving home, not going home."

IX
Airborne Warriors for the Working Day

The life of airborne infantrymen in Vietnam was at best drudgery---long, hard days of constant patrolling down jungle trails, across flooded rice paddies, up hills, and down ravines of various sizes and degrees of difficulty. They spent their nights on patrols and ambush positions or simply fighting to stay awake on perimeter guard until it was their turn to sleep. The drudgery was sometimes interrupted by climbing aboard hovering Hueys so they could be combat air assaulted into some LZ, possibly under enemy fire. And all this was accomplished while carrying 80 pounds or more of equipment.

An infantryman's life was, at best, drudgery

It's what troopers called "humping," a term used to describe the experience of being burdened down by those 80 pounds or so of gear, all day and all night, rain or shine.

Sunny days were mostly hot and oppressive, equipment heavy

under the broiling sun, fatigues soaked with sweat. Troopers chewed salt tablets all day long to fight off dehydration and heat prostration. The rainy days were always miserable, and equipment chafed into their skin over rain-drenched fatigues. The monsoon rains were relentless, and it sometimes seemed they would never end. Carrying 80 pounds of anything is difficult in the best of circumstances, and in combat it's even more difficult with the weather adding to the burden.

Load Bearing Equipment

The Army's solution to humping all this gear was the LBE, or load bearing equipment, which troopers nicknamed LBJ for load bearing junk. The load bearing equipment was a simple outfit that consisted of a harness worn over the shoulders that clipped onto the web belt in both the front and back. The web belt was worn waist high and it was for carrying ammo pouches, canteens, first aid kit, bayonet, and entrenching tools. On the front harness straps, troopers could also hang grenades, flashlights, compasses, and anything else they may need to access quickly. The back of the harness, hanging slightly below the shoulder blades, is where troopers carried their bedroll, which was important, because sleep was important.

Troopers got so little sleep that whatever sleep they did get was precious, and a good bedroll was essential. Most carried two camouflage-colored nylon blankets, called poncho liners, and many of them

It was important to keep your gear packed tight and dry

carried a 2-foot by 5-foot mat made of some sort of foam. Mats and blankets were rolled in a cylinder shape about 2 feet wide by about 8 inches thick, thicker if there were other items rolled in with the bedding, canned food being the most common; it also helped make a nice firm, round roll. Troopers then wrapped their rain ponchos over their entire bedrolls to protect them from the elements. Rolling bedding properly was important; it not only looked better, but a neat bedroll was less likely to snag on vines and branches as troopers moved through the bush. It also hung better and was easier to carry. The knapsacks were snapped onto their web belts and hung down their lower backs. Knapsacks carried chow, toiletries, letters from home, clean socks, underwear, extra ammo, and anything else that could cram into them.

In addition to the LBE, troopers carried canvas ammo bags with grenades, claymore mines, C4 explosives, detonating cord, and trip flares. They also carried disposable rocket launchers, called the LAW or light anti-tank weapon, which was used with good effect against bunkers and entrenched enemy positions. Everyone carried machine gun ammo; troopers could never have too much machine gun ammo, plus it looked cool having M-60 ammo bandoliers criss-crossed across your chest, real GI Joe sort of stuff.

A radio telephone operator's, burden was increased by another 30 pounds, the weight that was added by an AN/PRC-25 backpack radio, and the two extra batteries he was expected to carry.

The Crowning Touch of the Uniform

RTO Eddie Gatton

The crowning touch of a trooper's field uniform was his M-1 helmet, nicknamed the "steel pot." It was actually two helmets, the outer helmet stamped out of manganese steel, and the helmet liner, which was made of a compressed cotton resin that also contained an adjustable suspension system that could be fitted to various head sizes. Over the steel pot, troopers wore cloth camouflage helmet covers, which were jungle green with disruptive patterns. They also had slots cut in the cloth to allow troopers to stick in natural camouflage, such as twigs with leaves, shoots of jungle grass, and anything else that helped them blend in with the environment.

Veteran troopers adorned their helmets with graffiti

The camouflage cover was held in place by the helmet band that fit around the bottom of the headgear. The purpose of the cover was to hold additional camouflage, but it was mostly used as a carry-all to hold cigarettes, mosquito repellent, and additional ammo magazines. It was always easy to spot a new trooper because his helmet cover was bright green and free of graffiti; the camouflage covers of veteran troopers were bleached pale green by the sun and shrunk tight over the steel pot by the constant rain. The helmet covers of veteran old timers were also generally covered with graffiti, testifying to days in combat, days left in country, names of girlfriends, home towns, and various statements on the situation in general.

A Trooper's Combat Fatigues

Mike Friedrichs and Isaac Guest

All of this gear was worn over combat fatigues. Troopers who served with the 1st Air Cav in 1965 and early 1966 wore the traditional cotton fatigues and leather boots that they arrived with from stateside, until they rotted away. The jungle fatigues and jungle boots that were to become a familiar icon of the Vietnam War never made their way to the frontline troops until the spring of 1966. The rear echelon types all had jungle fatigues, and that was a big bone of contention with those in the infantry. It was justifiable resentment, especially when troopers came back to the An Khe base camp after a couple of weeks of humping in the jungle with their old stateside leather boots held together with all-purpose tape and commo wire and those stateside cotton fatigues literally disintegrating off their body, only to see some mail clerk drive by in a jeep wearing a new jungle uniform. It was a bit disconcerting. Life wasn't fair, especially in Vietnam.

Unfriendly Creatures in the Jungle

In addition to the NVA, troopers faced many other unfriendly creatures in that inhospitable jungle. Some walked, some crept, others slithered, and some even swung from trees. The jungles of Vietnam were a strange and exotic place with its thick triple-canopied jungle; it was spooky and beautiful at the same time.

"We had been beating the bush for several days, tracking an enemy unit,"recalls Sergeant Garry Bowles. "That evening we made camp in a company-sized perimeter, and after digging in and having chow, we settled in our positions. Everything was fine until about 2200 hours that night, and then directly in front of our position we started to receive incoming rocks and branches thrown at

The jungle was a strange and exotic place

us. Word was passed to hold our fire; sometimes the NVA would throw things at our positions, hoping we would fire our weapons and disclose our positions. We were bombarded all night long with rocks and branches, and, as dawn approached, the word was passed to throw grenades in the direction of the enemy. The grenades were thrown, and within seconds of the explosions subsiding, we heard this ear-splitting screeching followed by a rapid high-pitched chatter, and much to our surprise, sighted a big red orangutan swinging from tree to tree overhead of our positions. It gave me a true appreciation for the term 'guerrilla warfare.'"

As Lieutenant Ed Polonitza remembers, "Among the worst creatures encountered by the American soldier in Vietnam were the ugly brown leeches that somehow managed to invade every part of our bodies. No matter how much we tried, we couldn't keep the leeches from attaching themselves our arms, legs, and everywhere else, while gorging themselves fat with our blood. One ritual we performed whenever possible was stripping down and checking ourselves for leeches. We never ceased to be amazed where we would find them. No

matter how tightly we would lace our boots, we could find 10 or more leeches sucking onto our feet and ankles. I once heard a rumor that a trooper in one of our sister companies had a leech on his eyeball, and before it could be removed, he was blinded. I don't know whether this was true, but it sounded like something that could have happened. With trial and error, we learned to force the leeches to drop off our bodies by squirting them with lighter fluid or

Leeches, insects, and reptiles could be found on every jungle trail

by holding lit cigarettes against them. The leeches were disgusting, slimy, and unavoidable."

The jungle itself proved to be a formidable foe. There was a particularly pesky growth, known to troopers as a "wait a minute bush." As Specialist Mike Friedrichs recalls, "It was a vicious thing that was full of thorns and it had a curious way of wrapping

Evacuating Sergeant Johnson

around you, your weapon, and your equipment, as you moved through the jungle. There was no preventing being cut and scarred, as you tried to untangle yourself from its grasp."

Another horrendous plant was the elephant grass, which grew from 3 to 10 feet high with both sides of its broad leaves as sharp as a barber's razor. Troopers were constantly covered with scratches and cuts inflicted during encounters with the elephant grass.

Snakes were everywhere. It was not unusual to see various types of snakes in the trees, and slithering along the paths as troopers made their way through the dense jungles of the Central Highlands. Most snakes just got out of the way, but some were more aggressive. As Lieutenant Polonitza recalls, "On one combat patrol, the 3rd Platoon was deep in triple-canopy jungle with trees 40 to 50 feet high. As we were pushing our way through the underbrush, Sergeant Nathan Johnson suddenly dropped to his knees in great pain. I was immediately behind Johnson in the column and noticed a bright green snake slithering off a tree branch that Johnson had just brushed past. It was a highly poisonous bamboo viper. Sergeant Johnson's arm quickly swelled to the size of a balloon. Our platoon aid man administered first aid, but Johnson needed more medical assistance than we could provide. We radioed for a medevac helicopter, but the trees were so tall and dense that no landing zone was available. Our only option was an evacuation through the trees. We soon had a two-engine

Chinook helicopter hovering over our position. The jungle was so dense we could hear the chopper, but we couldn't see it. The pilot radioed us that he would drop a tethered basket through the trees, so we could load Sergeant Johnson into the basket, to be pulled into the Chinook. Fortunately for Sergeant Johnson, this exercise was successful, and he soon recovered fully from his poisonous bite."

Some of the worst enemies were the insects. Lieutenant Polonitza recalls putting his hand into a nest of fire ants during a night patrol. "My whole arm felt like it was on fire from the sting of the ants."

Specialist Mike Friedrichs recalled a jungle patrol where a young sergeant, fresh from the states, fell victim to an attack by a swarm of hornets: "We were patrolling up this jungle trail that crossed a little stream. The trail led across the stream and up a light rise. The new sergeant and I were bringing up the rear of the column; by the time we got across the stream, the incline of the trail was very muddy and slippery because of all the traffic in front of us. As we crossed the stream, I noticed a hornet's nest hanging from a low tree branch. The troopers in front of us all carefully ducked under the branch to avoid disturbing the hornets. The new sergeant lost his footing and slipped down the incline, his rifle catching the nest and dislodging it from the branch, provoking the wrath of hundreds of angry hornets, all attacking without mercy. His face and arms were completely covered with

Rain-flooded fields provided idea breeding ground for mosquitoes

puffy red swelling bumps, the worst of which were around his eyes. He was completely blinded by the attack. I managed to lead him away from the fallen nest and up the hill to safety where we were able to get him on a medevac chopper. He returned to us a week later none the worse for wear except for a lot of pink blotches on his face and arms."

However, by far, the creature that did the most damage was the mosquito. Vietnamese mosquitoes were nothing like the backyard barbecue variety found stateside. These guys were lethal, and they had the ability to cause malaria and dengue fever. Everyone carried mosquito repellent, but it did little good against these fearsome creatures. Troopers spent many miserable nights trying to cope with their biting and buzzing around their heads. This was one battle we generally lost. When Alpha Company troopers first arrived in Vietnam, they were told to beware of the Anopheles mosquito, which stands on its front legs to bite into the skin. Unfortunately, by the time they could detect its posture, it was generally too late. Malaria meant evacuation to Japan or to the hospital at Qui Nhon on the coast of the South China Sea. This is a horrendous disease marked by intermittent periods of chills and fever, which gradually develop into a continuous see-saw of violent chills and elevated fevers.

Like many troopers of A Company, Specialist Friedrichs had more than one bout of malaria. "The first time I had malaria," recounts Friedrichs, "was during operations along the Cambodian border in December of 1965. I was evacuated to the hospital at Qui Nhon, where, for two weeks, I slipped in and out of fever. The treatment I received consisted of heavy doses of electrolytes, quinine, and alcohol baths. I lost more than 20 pounds, and couldn't remember ever being that sick in my life. My second encounter came after being wounded in the hip during Operation Masher/White Wing. I was evacuated to the hospital in Japan, and, after several surgical procedures, I developed a high fever and chills. A blood smear was taken, which indicated malaria. My temperature spiked to a dangerous 105 degrees, and the fever continued for nearly a week. I recall hallucinating and awakening drenched in sweat. The sensation was like falling down a well and never hitting bottom; it was real fire and dragon stuff. It took me two months to recover from my hip wound and the malaria relapse. It was a humbling thought that a mosquito that weighed less than a finger nail clipping could bring me to my knees and do as much damage as that AK-47 round in my hip."

To combat the malaria epidemic, troopers began taking a daily white pill and a weekly pink one. No one knew what these were, but everyone remembers the morning ritual of the platoon medic distributing the pills and ensuring that everyone swallowed it. One battalion commander, with perhaps excessive faith in the pharmaceutical industry, threatened to court martial anyone in the battalion with malaria since this would be viewed as evidence of disobeying an order to take the daily and weekly pills. Even though the number of malaria cases declined once troopers started taking the pills, they were never totally effective, and malaria remained one of the major causes of American casualties during the war, with more than 40,000 soldiers being treated for the disease.

C-Rations

C-rations contained cigarettes, condiments, utensils, and more

Napoleon once said, "An Army travels on its stomach." The Alpha Raiders traveled on c-rations, the standard cuisine for the combat soldiers of the Vietnam War. Even today, most of them can recite the c-rations from memory. Each case had 12 meals. Even though they were c-rations, the meals, for some mysterious reason, were called B1, B2, and B3 units. Each contained a meat dish, fruit, and bread or dessert. Various meals included peanut butter, jam, and crackers. Each had an accessory packet with salt, pepper, gum, tissues, matches, plastic utensils, and cigarettes. In retrospect, the developer of these meals obviously didn't know, or perhaps didn't care, about a healthy diet. But, if one was doing what the Alpha Raiders were doing, it probably didn't matter anyway. Most preferred the B1 unit because it had a can of fruit.

Some c-rations were surpassingly tasty

In the heat of the jungle, anything with moisture was good. Nonsmokers would hoard their cigarette packets to trade for cans of fruit.

Some of the c-ration meals were not too bad. Beans and franks, chicken and noodles, and boned chicken tasted ok. Using its unique grammatical structure, the Army called one meal, "ham and eggs chopped," a favorite breakfast item. Several of the c-ration selections were barely edible. Ham and lima beans were eaten only if starvation was the alternative. Everyone had a P-38 can opener hanging from their dog tags. A P-38 was an ingenious device consisting of a tiny flat piece of metal with a hinged blade that opened a c-ration can in a flash. It was indestructible, convenient, and never failed on the job, undoubtedly the best can opener ever designed by man.

Grunts in the field are very innovative and creative in finding ways to establish any level of creature comfort. Most of the time, they ate their c-rations cold and right out of the can. Time was always pressing; fires of any type were a major security breach. But occasionally, conditions allowed troopers to heat up their meals. Some, like the ham and eggs chopped, were much better heated. Troopers sometimes received heat tablets to cook their meals.

The famous P-38 can opener

One creative and brave (or foolish) trooper discovered that C4, a high explosive carried to blow out landing zones or enemy bunkers, would burn with a very hot and intense flame, and thus was ideal for cooking purposes. This soon became the standard methodology until someone in the battalion supply section wanted an account of all the C4 being used.

There were some mysteries associated with our c-rations. The B1 unit included a round chocolate candy bar. For some reason, no matter how hot it got, the candy bars never melted, so we thought a great deal of scientific research must have gone into them. Unfortunately, the taste left something to be desired, but we doubted that good taste was the principal criterion placed before the manufacturer of these treats.

Over time, troopers discovered how to doctor up their c-rations to make them more palatable and less bland. Every soldier in the 3rd Platoon carried a bottle of hot sauce to spice up the menu. Soldiers all suspected that the war in Vietnam was very beneficial to the sales of the McIlhenny Company, manufacturer of tabasco sauce. In fact, the company published, *The Charlie Ration Cookbook* subtitled "No Food Is Too Good For The Man Up Front." As would be expected, most of the recipes featured the company's famous product.

Hot chow was always appreciated

Lieutenant Polonitza recalls personally hitting the wall on c-rations in October 1966: "After eating these every day for more than nine months, I had had enough. For the remaining several months of my tour, I subsisted on Slim Jims sent from home. Fortunately, back then we didn't know about cholesterol, trans-fats, and so on. We did occasionally have a break from the c-ration routine. We found that an M-79 grenade launcher is perfect for blowing coconuts out of trees. Once or twice we shot wild boars running through the jungle and found that when cooked they were a delicious treat. We even had hot meals in the field sometimes, which were greatly appreciated by the Airborne Warriors. Usually, these would be evening meals flown into our position by our resupply helicopter.

The army hot meals were what we call today 'comfort food,' mashed potatoes, green beans, and hamburger steaks, for example. Sometimes, we might have cake for dessert washed down with the army's famous green Kool-Aid.

On one occasion, our resupply helicopter had just brought a very welcome hot meal. After a tough day pushing through the jungle, the opportunity to semi-relax was irresistible. At the time, I was company executive officer, and one of my duties was to oversee the meal. As we were serving, a radio call came from our battalion headquarters ordering us to prepare for an immediate combat assault into a suspected enemy position. Captain Bouton told me to break down the serving line and dump the remaining food. Seeing all of our disappointed troopers, I asked if we could load up the food on one of our assault choppers and finish the meal at the landing zone. Captain Bouton agreed and off we went. As we assaulted into the LZ, troopers were firing M16s, machine guns, and our group was carrying containers of meat loaf. Fortunately, the LZ was free of any enemy, and we enjoyed the rest of our meal.

On one hot afternoon as we pushed through the boonies searching for the enemy, the company radios picked up traffic from a resupply chopper identifying itself as 'The Good Humor Man.' Since we were not expecting resupply, most of us ignored the squawking from our radios. Sensing an opportunity, the 1st Platoon leader, Tom Mancini, whose call sign was, ironically, 'Joker,' instructed his RTO, Andy Gerrier, call sign 'Joker India,' to guide the Good Humor Man to a secure clearing along our line of march. Soon enough we had an inbound chopper flaring into the LZ, dropping off five gallons of the most delicious ice cream any of us had ever tasted. Needless to say, the war stopped for us for a few minutes, but, unfortunately, this delightful treat was a one-time event. Sometimes the best efforts of our mess people didn't turn out as well as the ice cream event.

During an extended operation in Binh Dinh Province in the late spring, our higher command must have felt our c-ration diet was becoming monotonous. One day, rather than dropping off our normal resupply of c-rations, our logistics chopper kicked out cases of Vienna sausage. This became our diet for the next several days. I am sure that to this day, most of my fellow 3rd Platoon members have never again eaten another Vienna sausage."

Water was the beverage of choice for the grunts in the field. In fact, it was all they had available to drink. Each carried two quart-sized canteens. On a hot day, which was almost every day, and on a hard hump over rough terrain, which was also what troopers experienced almost every day, two quarts of water did not last long. One of the few advantages of operating in the mountain jungles of the Central Highlands was that troopers could find flowing streams to replenish their water. However, in the dry season, which ran from spring through summer, many of these streams dried up. The situation was even worse in the flat coastal plains, which were as dry as a bone for a good part of the year. In these circumstances, troopers were dependent on resupply helicopters for water, and, if these were unavailable for some reason, they did without. Sometimes in the brutally hot weather with no water available, the sludge in the rice paddies started to look refreshing. Troopers carried iodine tablets that supposedly purified the stagnant water they found in the streams, paddies, and ponds. No one ever knew whether the tablets did any good or not, but we did know the tablets gave the water a horrible taste they tried to overcome, to no avail, with Kool-Aid or lemonade powder.

Jungle Monsoons

Of all the things an infantryman had to cope with in Vietnam, the monsoon may have been the worst. The monsoon rains came at different times in different places in Vietnam. In the Central Highlands, the rains were at their peak from October through December. The rainy season of 1966 was repeatedly one of the worst in history. The rain was relentless and fell for several months without mercy, sometimes in a slow steady trickle, but most of the time, it fell in a steady mind-numbing downpour. Troopers ate in the rain, slept in the rain, patrolled in the rain, and sat all night long in ambush positions, perfectly still in the rain, hoping to surprise enemy patrols.

In addition to the very real psychological effects of being wet all the time, the monsoon also brought with it a special medical condition called immersion foot, which was called trench foot in previous wars. It was a painful affliction of the feet and lower extremities caused by prolonged exposure to wetness. Walking became extremely painful because feet would become puffy and spongy with terrible skin ulcers that would only heal by keeping the feet clean and dry, which was impossible during the monsoon.

At the beginning of the rainy season, Alpha Company troopers were conducting patrol operations in the central coastal plains of Binh Dinh Province. Their area of operation was distinguished by a series of dry riverbeds. The monsoon had just begun, and a light rain had been falling since the troops arrived. Several days into the operation, they found an area along a stretch of riverbed that appeared to be defensible and free of enemy activity, and with nightfall approaching, it appeared to be a good place to make camp. Once troopers had established their perimeter, they made poncho

The rain was relentless

shelters and prepared to settle in for the night.

Lieutenant Polonitza remembers, "One of my few concessions to comfort was an inflatable air mattress I carried in my bedroll. Once it was inflated, I laid down in my poncho hooch looking forward to a good night's sleep. The rain that had been falling lightly for several days gradually became more intense, and then suddenly turned into a torrential downpour. What had once been a dry riverbed suddenly turned into a raging torrent of water. My poncho shelter was washed away, and I found myself being washed downstream on my air mattress. The flash flood threw the entire company into disarray, weapons and equipment were being washed downstream, and men were scrambling for the safety of high ground. Fortunately for us, there was no enemy in the vicinity that night, or we would have been in big trouble. They were probably hiding in caves somewhere, comfortable and dry.

3rd Platoon choppers

Our mission in Binh Dinh Province continued into the month of December, and so did the rain. The monsoon and the effects of disease were taking a grim toll on the troopers of A Company. We were down to about 60 men total. Most of the rifle platoons, which were supposed to number 43 men and an officer, had been whittled down to fewer than a dozen men each. I was pulling double duty leading the 3rd Platoon in addition to my job as company executive officer. Despite the lack of men, we were still expected to continue our mission of finding and destroying the enemy, so we all soldiered on in true airborne fashion. Late one afternoon, we received a radio call ordering us to find an LZ and prepare for extraction. Normally, it took six choppers to lift a rifle platoon, but because of our depleted state, it could now be done with only two. As we waited on the LZ for our choppers, someone mentioned it was Christmas Eve. To us in that LZ, it had been just another day; the spirit of Christmas was just a memory from a time long ago in a place far away. The choppers approached, and we popped smoke grenades to mark our location. We climbed aboard the Hueys for the ride to our next air assault position. We approached the LZ, which was a wide white sandy beach on the shore of the South China Sea. Upon landing, we set up a defensive perimeter around a cluster of palm trees within sight of the ocean. It was raining steadily, and darkness was approaching, so we were all anxious to dig in before nightfall. The good news was that the next day we were to stand down from combat operations in honor of a Christmas truce that had been declared by our high command in Saigon. We wondered if the NVA had gotten the word; we all hoped so.

The next morning, as the sun rose over the South China Sea, an amazing thing happened. As if by some miracle, the rain suddenly stopped, and the morning sky was filled with a warm and nurturing sun. We all laid our wet clothes and equipment on the beach to dry; troopers sprawled on the sand in their shorts soaking up the warmth from the sun. We hung grenades and ammo belts around a small evergreen tree, and it suddenly started to feel like Christmas. Early that afternoon, we got the word that a chopper was inbound to our location with Christmas dinner and all the fixings. The meal was wonderful; it was as if the gods of war were paying tribute to the men of A Company by granting us this special time. For a while we all felt like human beings again.

The following morning, the choppers arrived at our seaside resort, and we regretfully loaded aboard them, back to the dark canopied jungle of Binh Dinh Province, for an air assault. As the Hueys approached the LZ for our assault, the sky became overcast, and, as we leapt from the hovering choppers to resume our mission, it began to rain. Once again, we were but warriors for the working day."

The End of An Era

A few days later Lieutenant Polonitza got the word that within the week he would be returning stateside. The Lieutenant was a member of the "old guard," and one of the few remaining troopers who was jump qualified. The entire battalion had been taken off jump status in November. His departure brought to an end the era of the Alpha Airborne Warriors.

Alpha Airborne Warriors Remembered

Nearly forty years have passed since the Airborne Warriors of A Company, 2nd Battalion (Airborne), 8th Cavalry prowled the jungles of Central Highlands of Vietnam. None of us will ever forget the great soldiers who made up that proud unit. Together, we endured some of the toughest conditions an infantryman can experience. We recall every day the heavy loads we humped, the mountains we climbed, the jungle we hacked our way through, the never ending rain that drenched us, and the diseases that afflicted us. When we met the enemy, we fought on our terms, not theirs, and always gave better than we got. We still can remember the exhilaration of standing on the strut of a Huey, our weapons at the ready, as we air assaulted into a hot LZ under enemy fire. Combat is something you never forget. Thankfully, the years have gentled the memories of those times and the hardships we experienced.

Most of all, we remember our comrades, whose names are carved in the Wall and those who have left us since our return, each a brother, a father, a husband, or son; they are with us always, in Honor and Courage.

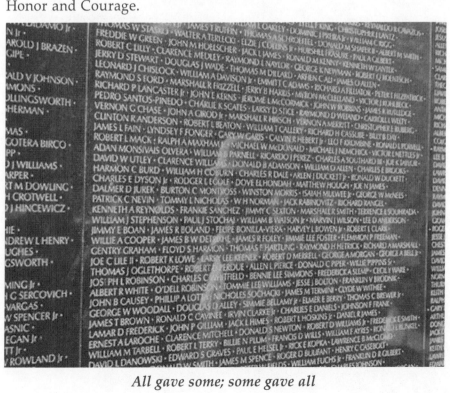

All gave some; some gave all

X
Epilogue

Leonard Lawrence serving with the 82nd Airborne in 1967, in Vietnam in 1965, and with his Veterans of Foreign Wars troop in 1998.

In the early summer of 1966, those Alpha Raiders who had arrived in Vietnam on the USNS *Geiger* the previous summer began returning stateside. By the following January, the last of the original Airborne Warriors returned home to the land of the big PX. Most of them ended up in the 82nd Airborne Division at Fort Bragg, North Carolina, or the

101st Airborne at Fort Campbell, Kentucky. Those who were assigned to the 82nd, and had more than a year left on their enlistments, soon found themselves back in Vietnam just in time for the Tet Offensive of February 1968. Both Specialist Juan Fernandez and Specialist Mike Friedrichs returned to Vietnam with the 82nd for Tet, which, unlike most other battles, was named for a time, not a place.

"I returned home stateside in November of 1966," recalls Sergeant Garry Bowles. "I requested, and was granted, an additional 10 days on my scheduled 30-day leave from the Army, so that I might enjoy both the Thanksgiving and Christmas holidays at home. I had no sooner arrived when I started to experience chills and fevers. I was soon gripped with vomiting and diarrhea and knew beyond any shadow of a doubt that I was having a relapse of malaria. I was rushed by ambulance to a nearby military hospital, where I spent both Thanksgiving and Christmas recovering. Mine was not a unique experience. Most who had contracted this terrible disease suffered relapses upon their return stateside."

Lieutenant Ed Polonitza returned to the States, and, after a three-month hospital stay recovering from malaria, was assigned to the Mountain Ranger Camp at Dahlonega, Georgia, as a Ranger instructor. Ed's time as an instructor was short lived, as he also returned to Vietnam and saw service during Tet with the 101st Airborne Division. Staff Sergeant Isaac Guest returned to Vietnam and served as an advisor to the South Vietnamese Army. Isaac stayed in the service and retired as a sergeant major, the highest enlisted rank. Captain Tom Forman, Alpha Company Commander during several of our most significant battles, also served as an advisor during a second tour. Sergeant Duke DuShane later served with distinction in a number of senior enlisted capacities with Papa Company of the 75th Rangers, which performed long-range combat and reconnaissance patrols throughout

Sergeant Duke DuShane was inducted into the Ranger Hall of Fame

Vietnam. Several years ago, "The Duke" was inducted into the Ranger Hall of Fame, a well-deserved honor.

The Tet Offensive

Walter Cronkite

Unfortunately, those who served subsequent tours to the war zone found they were not as fulfilling or rewarding as the first. Two events conspired to negate the heroic efforts of the infantrymen who fought the war, which eventually made them realize their efforts would be for naught. The first was the Tet Offensive of 1968. For the American soldiers on the ground in Vietnam, this battle was a tremendous victory. All over the country, Viet Cong and North Vietnamese forces were totally destroyed. In fact, after Tet, the Viet Cong ceased permanently to be an effective fighting force. The NVA was unable to mount any subsequent major efforts until 1972, shortly after the departure of the bulk of the American combat units. Unfortunately, this was not how the events surrounding Tet were perceived by the American media.

"I was in the 101st Airborne Division in early 1968," recalls Lieutenant Polonitza. "We had been fully alerted by our intelligence people that a major enemy offensive was planned and were fully prepared when the NVA struck. After the horrendous defeat we had inflicted on the enemy, morale was sky high. We were thinking that the war would soon be over, and we would be going home for good. I was shocked when we began to receive the press reports from back in the States. *Newsweek* magazine ran an extensive editorial; the first in the magazine's history, exhorting the prowess of the NVA and declaring that a terrible defeat had been inflicted on the American military. CBS anchorman, Walter Cronkite continued the defeatist theme. In a report he gave following the Tet Offensive, he declared, 'The war was unwinnable, and the United States would have to find a way out.'"

Those who fought in the Tet Offensive knew the truth and were appalled that the facts could be so misinterpreted by the press and misunderstood by the American people. This became the theme adopted by the press and certain politicians. In May of 1969, when elements of the 101st Airborne were fighting the battle of Ap Bia Mountain, or Hamburger Hill, Senator Edward Kennedy, in a speech on the floor of the Senate, scorned the American military and condemned the battle as "senseless and irresponsible," and declared, "the hill couldn't be taken." The grunts of the 101st apparently disagreed and took the hill and utterly defeated the defending NVA forces only to be defeated by the media once again as it portrayed American victories as defeats.

Media Opposition

Not the least of the slurs on the American fighting men was Jane Fonda's visit to North Vietnam and the shameful picture of her smiling as she sat in the gunner's chair of an enemy anti-aircraft gun. This weapon was deployed to kill American pilots. We fault less the NVA gunners who actually used these guns in combat because they were professional soldiers fighting a war. Jane Fonda's treasonous pose, however, was no less than contemptible, as it encouraged and glorified our country's enemies.

The attacks and distortions continued, even as the American military was being withdrawn from Vietnam. On January 31, 1971, members of Vietnam Veterans Against the War met in Detroit to document war crimes that they had participated in or witnessed during their combat tours in Vietnam. Over the next three days, more than 100 Vietnam veterans and civilians gave anguished, emotional testimony describing hundreds of atrocities against innocent civilians in South Vietnam, including rape, arson, torture, murder, and the shelling or napalming of entire villages.

Jane and friends posing with an anti-aircraft gun
used to shoot down American pilots

Ted Kennedy and John Kerry at a war protest

The witnesses stated that these acts were being committed casually and routinely, under orders, as a matter of American military policy. In April, they stormed Washington in a week-long protest.

At its height, spokesman John Kerry went before the Senate Committee on Foreign Relations to accuse the United States military of committing massive numbers of was crimes in Vietnam. The appearance launched Kerry's political career. The charges he made shocked and sickened a nation and stained the reputation of the American military for decades. But the mass murder of civilians was never American policy in Vietnam. War crimes were the exception, not the rule. And the so called "Winter Soldier Tribunal," which Kerry helped moderate, turned out to be, in the words of historian Guenter Lewy, "packed with pretenders and liars."

Looking back over the history of our country, we can give thanks that the media and politicians at the time of Valley Forge, Antietam, and the Battle of the Bulge had different perspectives than the opinion makers of the late 1960s. If the press of those past eras had misconstrued the facts and events, as did the media during the Vietnam War, America may not have survived those previous conflicts.

LBJ Abandons the War Effort

A second event shaping the grunt's perspective on the war also occurred in 1968. This was President Johnson's announcement in the spring of that year that he would not run for reelection. Many said that Johnson reached this decision as a result of Walter Cronkite's denounce-

Kerry testifies about "so-called war crimes"

ment of the war. David Halberstam, the Pulitzer Prize-winning journalist of the *New York Times*, wrote, "It was the first time in American history a war had been declared over by an anchorman." The soldiers on the ground felt the rug had been pulled out from under them. If the country's Commander-in-Chief could not take the heat from the media and the political process, what chance did the soldiers have of success? They felt the blood, tears, and sweat they had shed were meaningless contributions to the whims of Washington politicians. They looked back in history at strong, resolute leaders, like Washington, Lincoln, and Roosevelt, and cursed our fate to be led by contemptible weaklings, like Johnson and McNamara, who lacked the courage and commitment of the grunts they sent to fight and die in the Vietnam War. But soldiers continued to soldier on even though they knew the outlook was grim and the sacrifice was unappreciated.

Back to Civilian Life

The great majority of the Airborne Warriors of Alpha Company returned stateside, and when their enlistments were completed, they returned to civilian life. Like the rest of mainstream America, they went to school, married, started families and careers, and melted slowly into what became known as the great silent majority. Over the years, a few kept in touch, and several years ago, they began using the Internet to track down comrades from so many years ago. "Several years ago," recalls Lieutenant Ed Polonitza, "Garry Bowles, our intrepid company medic and pony soldier, created an Alpha Company roster at his Kensington Pond

McNamara and Johnson---architects of defeatism

Books web site. A number of A Company veterans located old buddies through this web site, and some powerful memories returned."

Private First Class Joe Brown, the 17-year-old artillery forward observer, who became a hero of A Company's first flight with the NVA on November 4, 1965, discovered this online roster while surfing the net. During the November 4th battle, Joe calmly called in a ferocious artillery barrage while under heavy enemy fire. His fire mission broke the back of the enemy attack and stopped the enemy assault. Tragically, one of the friendly artillery rounds fell short, killing or wounding a number of A Company troopers. Joe was devastated at the carnage the short round had inflicted on his buddies. He was overwhelmed with guilt and a sense of personal responsibility for this event. In his Bible, Joe wrote the names of those killed and carried the memory of that day for the next 40 years. As he scanned the Alpha Company roster hoping to find the names of old friends, one name jumped out at him. The name was Art Miller, one of the names in his Bible. Joe couldn't believe it. He sent an email message to the address next to the name.

Joe asked, "Are you the Art Miller who was with the 3rd Platoon during the November 4th battle?"

"Yes," was the reply. "I'm that Art Miller."

Art had been wounded, but not killed, by the errant artillery round. Joe asked for Art's telephone number and they talked for hours. Joe felt that a small part of the burden from that day 40 years ago had been lifted from him. Despite his guilt, all present during that battle consider Joe to be a hero. Apparently so did the Army. Joe was awarded the Bronze Star with "V" device for his heroism that day. He was one of the youngest soldiers in the Vietnam War to receive that decoration.

Events from that time 40 years ago come full circle in many different ways. John Spranza was one of the few survivors of the NVA attack on LZ Hereford in May 1966. He was discharged from the Army as a sergeant after recovering from the wounds he received during the battle on Hereford. One never forgets an event as traumatic as his experience in that small place. Just before Christmas of 2004, nearly 40 years later, John received a package in the mail that brought back vivid memories of that terrible day in May 1966. The return address on the package was not familiar to him. It was from Stacy Hansen of California. In the package was the dog tag Spranza was wearing on the day of the NVA attack. Ms. Hansen had recently been traveling in Vietnam and came across a street vendor selling war-era dog tags purportedly worn by American soldiers. She bought a group of these dog tags and made extraordinary efforts to return them to their original owners. John Spranza has no idea how his dog tag got in the hands of the Vietnamese street vendor. Perhaps it was cut from his neck by a North Vietnamese soldier during the attack or lost during his medical evacuation out of Vietnam. In any event, this lost dog tag has become a cherished reminder of his service and of his heroic last stand on LZ Hereford.

Joe Brown and Art Miller at the 2005 summer reunion

"To date, 30 former Alpha Raiders have been found alive and well," reports Sergeant Bowles. "A dozen more are known to have died since their return from the war, many from causes attributed to Agent Orange. The Vietnam War continues to take its toll on the paratroopers of Alpha Company. Tom Forman, the much-liked and well-respected company commander of the Alpha Raiders, died in 1993 at the age of 58 from cancer of the larynx caused by Agent Orange exposure. All of us who went up Hospital Hill on February 27, 1966, will always remember his skill,

Tom Forman, shortly before his death in 1993

courage, and calm leadership under fire that day. The news of this fine man's death saddened us all.

Like many of my old comrades, I often think of my time as an Airborne Warrior. I recall those days with great pride and a certain longing, as if by remembering, I can somehow turn back the clock and capture a fragment of my long lost youth.

Over the years many have asked, 'Why did you fight? Was it patriotism? The mom-and-apple-pie thing? Was it brotherhood? Did you fight for each other? Or was it a macho thing, the need to be tested in combat and not found wanting?'

Our reply is 'Yes, it was all those things and more.'

At the heart of it was the paratrooper mystique, the common bond we shared as Airborne Warriors. We took for granted that as paratroopers we were expected to march further and fight harder than the ordinary soldiers that we disparagingly called 'legs.' We were considered to be elite troops, and were proud of the fact that much was expected of us. Our paratrooper training taught us more than just how to jump out of airplanes. It taught us how to manage fear and to function, despite the terror of combat. We were trained to fight and win. Defeat was not in our creed. Our confidence in battle was born of the fact that we had all undergone the same rigorous training, and, as paratroopers, we were men who could be counted on in the cauldron of combat. We were then, and remain still, 'Airborne all the way!'"

Left to right: Garry Bowles, Leonard Lawrence, Ed Polonitza, Juan Fernandez, Bill Garlinger, Jim Rockwell, and Isaac Guest

Home at Last

*This is a tribute to those Alpha Airborne Raiders,
and this proudly is their story.*

*The memories of those once-young men,
a story of their honor, a saga of their glory.*

*From the border of Cambodia to Tuy Hoa and Bong Son,
the Mang Yang Pass to Pleiku,*

*The Alpha Raiders of long ago, the young men who fought that war,
they did it all for you.*

*So if by chance, someday while standing on parade,
you see those Raiders pass,*

*Please bow your head and thank your God
that they've all come home at last.*

---Garry Bowles

Acknowledgements

In September 1965 a group of young paratroopers came ashore from the waters of the South China Sea and across the beaches of Qui Nhon into the country of Vietnam. For the next 15 months these men and their successors fought in some of the bloodiest campaigns of the Vietnam War against a relentless and dangerous enemy. When their year-long tours ended, they went home. Some stayed in the army and returned to Vietnam for second tours in the war zone. Most left the military and went about their lives. Over the years, they drifted apart but all retained the memories and thoughts of those exhilarating yet frightening experiences of their year at war. We never forgot our fellow troopers who fought bravely at our side. We never forgot those who fell in our battles, young men forever. As we grow old, the urge to reconnect with this formative time of our lives becomes more intense. *Honor and Courage* is inspired by an effort to recall and commemorate the experiences of our year at war and to bring together once again the Airborne Warriors of Alpha Company, 2nd Battalion (Airborne) 8th Cavalry.

Those of us responsible for preparing this history are by no measure, professional writers. We are simple combat soldiers who saw a need to preserve the history of a unique military unit that existed as an elite airborne/airmobile infantry outfit for only a short period of time. We hope the reader will forgive our lack of literary sophistication and enjoy the passion and realism with which we tried to tell our story. Unlike other stories of Vietnam combat, we refuse to agonize or whine about our experiences. We recall them with a sense of accomplishment and a sense of achievement toward the noble cause of keeping the people of South Vietnam free from Communist dictatorship. Although this goal was not achieved in the long run, we know this was not due to any shortcoming on our part, but rather to the weakness and failures of the political leaders of that time.

As we write our memories of that time 40 years ago and recall those who fought with us, we think of the words of Henry V to his soldiers on the eve of the battle of Agincourt:

> For he today that sheds his blood with me
> Shall be my brother; be he ne'er so vile,
> This day shall gentle his condition:
> And gentlemen in England, now a-bed
> Shall think themselves accursed they were not here

All of us who were involved in creating *Honor and Courage* would like to honor the memory of Lieutenant Colonel (Retired) J.D. Coleman. J.D. was buried on October 10, 2005, near his home in Kalispell, Montana. As a young captain, he commanded B Company of our battalion during the ferocious battles of Operation Crazy Horse in May 1966. He served a second tour with the 1st Cavalry in 1969 as Division Public Information Officer. He was considered by many to be the final authority on Air Cavalry history. His two best-known published works are *Pleiku, the Dawn of Helicopter Warfare in Vietnam* and *Incursion*. These two books have become mandatory reading for those interested in the history of airmobile warfare in Vietnam.

Over the past several years, we have located a number of former A Company paratroopers. Fifteen have contributed individual stories of their time as Airborne Warriors. Many also contributed actual combat after action reports, copies of orders for awards and decorations, company rosters, organizational charts, and various icons of the Vietnam War. These included Vietnamese money, military payment certificates, American and North Vietnamese propaganda leaflets, the Tabasco Company c-ration cookbook, and our Christmas 1966 dinner menu with General Westmoreland's holiday message. We also received hometown newspaper articles about Alpha Company along with clippings from the national press and hundreds of photographs.

We would like to extend our special thanks to the Airborne Warriors of A Company who helped make *Honor and Courage* their book. They are in alphabetical order: Joe Brown, Dave Dement, Duke Dushane, Alex Dziekonski, Juan Fernandez, Mike Friedrichs, Bill Garlinger, Isaac Guest, Joe Holtslag, Leonard Lawrence, Art Miller, Jim Rockwell, Sid Shearing, Marty Stango, and Erle Taylor. Others who made major contributions include Carole Cornett, who shared with us the story of her brother, 1st Lieutenant Don Cornett, who was killed at the battle of LZ Albany. Carole's story recalls the sad homecoming of her brother and his burial at Arlington Cemetery.

Fellow "All the Way" Brigade veteran John Spranza of Charlie Company, 1st Battalion (Airborne) 12th Cavalry, was kind enough to share his recollections of a horrific day on LZ Hereford when our A Company arrived too late to save his mortar platoon from virtual annihilation at the hands of an overwhelming North Vietnamese force. Captain Ted Danielsen helped us with the story of the Alphagators of 1st Battalion (Airborne) 8th Cavalry's historic first ever night air assault into a hot landing zone during the Pleiku campaign. Our special thanks go to other Jumping Mustangs of the 1st of the 8th including their battalion commander, Colonel (Retired) Ken Mertel and Colonel (Retired) Jack Peevy for their encouragement and comments. A special thank you to our former battalion commander, Major General (Retired) John Hemphill for his leadership then and his guidance and support in our endeavors now.

Gratitude and appreciation to George Cook for his excellent Air Cav illustrations, and to his sister Jeanie, who spent painstaking hours producing the actual story and accompanying websites. Thanks to Christy Boyer who did our transcriptions and produced the book's index. Last, and certainly not least, our gratitude goes to Donna Louise Ferrier who provided the final proofreading, editing, design, and formatting which brought everyone's efforts and contributions into a publication of which we are all proud. For their extraordinary contribution to *Honor and Courage,* they deserve and have been designated honorary "Alpha Airborne Raiders."

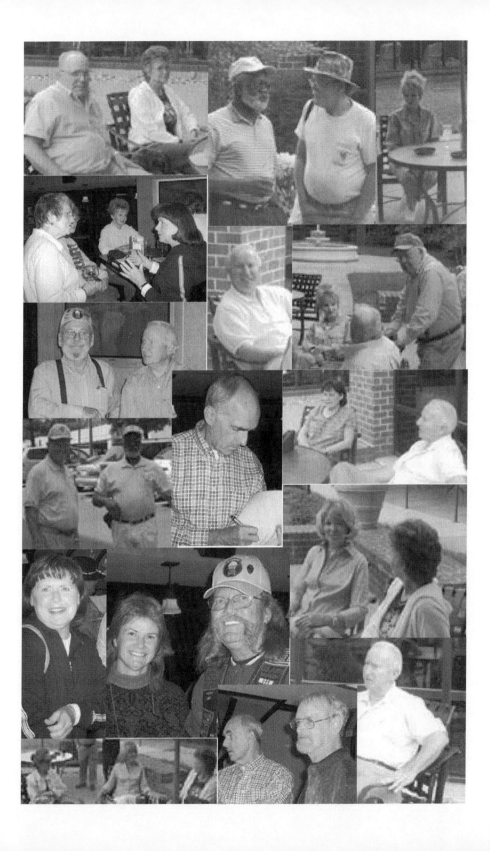

Appendix I
Alpha Company Rosters

George Orwell once wrote, "We sleep safely in our beds because rough men stand ready in the night to visit violence on those who would do us harm."

On August 20, 1965, 169 brave and determined men boarded the USNS *Geiger* bound for Vietnam. Over the next 31 days, their voyage took them through the Panama Canal, across the Pacific Ocean and into the port of Qui Nhon, South Vietnam. During the journey into battle, Specialist Billie Brandenburg, Alpha Company's administrative clerk, prepared a roster of those present for duty. Over the next year, many of these young paratroopers would be killed or wounded in action. Specialist Brandenburg's roster is the only existing document identifying the initial members of Alpha Company who began the unit's seven years spent visiting violence on North Vietnamese and Viet Cong soldiers in many bloody battles.

Note: The appendices have been reproduced exactly as they were written in 1965-1966 and do contain typographical errors and misspellings.

COMPANY "A"
2D BATTALION (AIRBORNE), 8TH CAVALRY
1ST CAVALRY DIVISION (AIRMOBILE)
APO SAN FRANCISCO, CALIFORNIA, 96490

COMPANY HEADQUARTERS

COMPANY COMMANDER	CAPT FORMAN
EXECUTIVE OFFICER	1ST LT MIKLAS
FIRST SERGEANT	1ST SGT MOORE
SUPPLY SERGEANT	SGT KRAUSE
COMMO CHIEF	SGT HOSEL
COMPANY CLERK	SP4 BRANDENBURG
COMPANY ARMORER	SP4 THURSTON
* SUPPLY CLERK	SP4 BOYCE
RADIO MACHANIC	SP4 RAMIREZ
RTO	PFC GATTON
RTO	PFC PASTRANO
WIREMAN	PFC MARSHALL
* OPERATIONS SGT	SP4 BUNSTON
* TNG CLERK	SP4 OPELA

FIRST PLATOON

PLATOON LEADER	2/LT STANGO
PLATOON SERGEANT	PSO AHN
RTO	PVT SYKORA

1ST SQUAD	2ND SQUAD	3RD SQUAD
SL SSG WILLIAMS	SL SSG LESTER	SL SSG KELLING
TL SGT DEUERLING	L SGT SANTIAGO	TL SP5 LEWIS
AR PFC THOMAS	AR PFC JACKSON, A	AR PFC WILLIFORD
G SP4 FORTENBERRY	G PVT EDWARDS	G PFC BUTLER
RL PFC BLACKMON	RL PVT MALLOE RL	PFC COFFMAN
TL SGT CAV	TL SGT BEATTY TL	SGT THORNTON
AR PFC HERRING	AR SP4 THORNTON	AR SP4 PERRY
G PFC HAIDET	G PFC WADE	G PFC BONE
R PFC SHEARING	R PVT MILLER	R PFC CHANDLER
R PVT HANSEN		R PVT LOWE

WEAPONS SQUAD

SL SSG ROACH	1/90 PFC HUGHES
A/SL SGT KUHNKE	A/90 PFC JACKSON, L
1/MG PFC TANKSLLY	2/90 PVT WELSH
A/NO PFC LESLIE	A/90 PVT SOLAS
2/MG PVT DELGADO	A/B PVT STOEFFLER
A/MG PVT THARP ***	A/B PVT GAMBLE

(*) NOT TO&E
(***) READ DETACHEMENT

COMPANY "A"
2D BATTALION (AIRBORNE), 8TH CAVALRY
1ST CAVALRY DIVISION (AIRMOBILE)
APO SAN FRANCISCO, CALIFORNIA, 96490

2ND PLATOON

PLATOON LEADER	LT PARRACK
PLATOON SERGEANT	PSO CARRERA
RTO	PFC BALLARD

1ST SQUAD	2ND SQUAD	3RD SQUAD
SL SSG LOWMAN	SL SSG HARVEY	SL SSG LINSEY
TL SGT BAKER	TL SGT LANE	TL SGT SAVAGE
AR PVT STEWART	AR PFC AUSTIN	AR PVT BOYKIN
G PFC FAUST	G PFC LUNA	G SP4 WOODY
RL PVT MARTINEZ, M	RL PVT RUSSO	RL PFC TAYLOR
TL SGT BEGIN	TL SGT SMITH R	TL SGT SPENCER
AR PFC BRADLEY	AR PVT BELLIVSAU	AR PVT SNYDER
G CPL BROWN	G SP4 ORAHAM	G PVT ESCOBAR
R PFC MARTINEZ, J	R PFC MERRELL	R PFC HOMMER

WPNS SQUAD

SL SSG BERGEN
HO SP4 FRULLANEY
A/MG PVT EVANS
MG SP4 SPESSARD
A/MG PVT GARLINGER
90G PVT JOHNSON J
A900 PVT TINDER
90G PVT SWARTZFAGER
A/90G PFC FRASIER
AB PFC RICH
AB PVT MAHONEY

EXCESS   SSG HARRIS

COMPANY "A"
2D BATTALION (AIRBORNE), 8TH CAVALRY
1ST CAVALRY DIVISION (AIRMOBILE)
APO SAN FRANCISCO, CALIFORNIA, 96490

3RD PLATOON

PLATOON LEADER   LT MARR\
PLATOON SERGEANT   PSG WELCH
RTO   PFC HILL

1ST SQUAD	2ND SQUAD	3RD SQUAD
SL SSG FLOREZ	SL SSG MILLS	SL SSG GUEST
TL SGT JARZENSKI	TL SGT JOHNSON, R	TL SGT HESTER
AR PFC BOOZE	AR PVT GRANKO	AR PFC MCINNIS
G SP4 JOHNSON	G SP4 LONG	G PFC HAWKINS
R PFC GLASS	R PVT LUKE	R PFC LAWRENCE
TL SGT MILLER	TL SGT WEBB	TL SGT TANKSLEY
AR SP4 QUIGLEY	G SP4 FERNADEZ	AR PVT COLON
G PVT BALDWIN	G SP4 GRANVILLE	G SP4 JOHNSON
R PFC FERNANDEZ	R PVT BARNETT	R PFC BLACKWOOD
R PFC CANCEL	R SP4 TRAMMELL	R PFC LEAKS

WPN SQUAD

SL SSG DAILEY
MG PFC GOLDSMITH
A/MG PVT DANIELS
MG PFC SMITH
A/MG PVT MOORE
90G PVT DEMENT
A/900 PFC BARTH
90G PVT SINGLETON
A/90G PVT TOWNSEND
AB PVT TRUJILLE
AB PVT WILSON

EXCESS   SFC FAIRLEY
                        SP4 BUNSTON

COMPANY "A"
2D BATTALION (AIRBORNE), 8TH CAVALRY
1ST CAVALRY DIVISION (AIRMOBILE)
APO SAN FRANCISCO, CALIFORNIA, 96490

WEAPONS PLATOON

PLATOON LEADER	LT TAYLOR
PLATOON SERGEANT	SSG SCHAER
RTO-1	PFC FINLEY
RTO-2	PFC SASRGENT
1ST FO	SGT LAMKIN
2ND FO	SGT ARKLESS
3RD FO	SGT BRADLEY
1ST FDC	SGT BOYER
2ND FDC	SP4 MCGRAW
3RD FDC	

1ST SQUAD	2ND SQUAD	3RD SQUAD
SL SGT LIVINGSTON	SL SGT EDWARDS	SL SGT DUNCAN
G PFC SCULAC	G PFC RICHARDSON	G SP4 WADDELL
A/G PFC MASUCCI	A/G PFC TENNYSON	A/G PFC RITCHIE
AB PVT HERRON	AB PVT WILLIAMS	AB PVT WEBB
AB PVT NIXON	AB PVT SPENCER	AB PVT WHIPPLE
AB PVT CARRERAS	AB PVT MAJOR	AB PVT DEVORE

CONFIDENTIAL
SOI ITEM 60A-3

2/8 CAV RIGHT HALF CMD	A.	*35.30
	B.	*60.65
A/LOG		*68.85
A CO. RIGHT GUARD		*68.55
B CO. RIGHT TACKLE		*67.95
C CO. RIGHT END		*67.25
D CO. FLANKER RIGHT		*65.85
AT. BUCKEYE		*65.45
MTR. BOILER MAKER		*57.35
RCN. WILD CAT		*55.45
RIGHT HALF LIFT		*30.50

An old cliche notes, "There are no atheists in foxholes." When the paratroopers of the 1st Brigade returned to the base camp at An Khe from combat operations, unit commanders focused on after-action reports, replenishing supplies and equipment, training replacements, and planning the next offensive. For the young soldiers of the brigade, this was a time to think about those buddies who did not return, to contemplate their own mortality, and, for many, a time to seek spiritual support. Fortunately for these young troopers, the 1st Brigade was blessed with an outstanding group of chaplains, many of whom had previous experience as enlisted soldiers and who had a keen understanding of the spiritual needs of these men; for example, Chaplain Bill Lord, of the 1st Battalion (Airborne) 12th Cavalry, was an infantry sergeant with the 11th Airborne Division before being ordained to the ministry. Chaplain Lord was awarded the Silver Star Medal for his heroic actions during Operation Shiny Bayonet in October 1965. In this photo, he baptizes a young cavalryman in a stream somewhere in the Ia Drang Valley in November 1965. Chaplain Lord baptized a number of 1st Brigade soldiers including Dave Dement, one of Alpha Company's Airborne Warriors.

Appendix II
Daily Staff Journals

Every army unit of battalion size and larger is required to maintain a staff duty officer log during combat operations. These logs are meant as a historic record of the interaction among the recording unit and the higher and lower organizations in its chain of command. The duty officer logs shown in the appendix are the actual records kept during 2nd Battalion (Airborne) 8th Cavalry's initial contact with the North Vietnamese Army in early November 1965. While generally very terse and concisely written, these documents provide an indication of the flow of the ongoing battle and the battalion's headquarters response to the action on the ground.

ORGANIZATION OR INSTALLATION LOCATION   PERIOD COVERED

		FROM		TO	
		HOUR	DATE	HOUR	DATE
S3, 2/8, CAV	FWD CP	0001	04 NOV 65	2400	04 NOV 65

ITEM NO	TIME IN	OUT	INCIDENTS, MESSAGES, ORDERS, ETC	ACTION TAKEN	INL
1			JOURNAL OPENED 040001 NOV 65		
2		0001	BDE: SIT REP - NEG		
3	0003		D: SIT REP - NEG		
4	0005		C: SIT REP - NEG		
5	0100		A: SIT REP - NEG		
6	0102		B: SIT REP - NEG		
7		0105	BDE CO: SIT REP - NEG		
8	0200		A CO: SIT REP - NEG		
9	0201		B CO: SIT REP - NEG		
10		0205	BDE CO: SIT REP - NEG		
11		0300	BDE CO: SIT REP – NEG		
12	0301		A CO: SIT REP - NEG		
13	0304		B CO: SIT REP - NEG		
14	0315		C CO: SIT REP – NEG		
15	0230		INFORMED WE WOULD NOT GET AIRCRAFT AS PLANNED		
16		0415	BDE: SIT REP - NEG		
17	0410		A: SIT REP - NEG		
18	0421		B: SIT REP - NEG		
19	0430		BDE 6 TO COL NIX: LOCATE LZ AND SECURE FOR ARTY AT FIRST LIGHT VIC N/S GL 90. 1/9 IS IN TROUBLE AND MUST COMMIT 1/8 VIC ENP 3462 (834062)		
20		0600	BDE CO: SIT REP – NEG		
21	0601		A CO: SIT REP – NEG		
22	0642		B CO: SIT REP – NEG		

PED NAME AND GRADE OF OFFICER OR OFFICIAL OH DUTY SIGNATURE

FORM 1594

ORGANIZATION OR INSTALLATION LOCATION   PERIOD COVERED

			FROM		TO	
			HOUR	DATE	HOUR	DATE
S3, 2/8, CAV		FWD CP	0001	04 NOV 65	2400	04 NOV 65

ITEM NO	TIME IN	OUT	INCIDENTS, MESSAGES, ORDERS, ETC	ACTION TAKEN	INL
23	0800		C CO: LEFT CAVALAIR BASE		
24	0830		C CO: TOUCHDOWN AT		
25	0846		C CO: 2D ELEM LEFT CAVALAIR BASE		
26	0855		C CO: 2D ELEM TOUCHDOWN AT		
27	0930		B CO: CLOSED AT AMY		
28	0950		BDE: C CO IS ATTACHED TO 1/8		
29	1015		RECON PLAT: ELEM HAS CONTACTED ENEMY		
30			RECON PLAT: CAPTURED ONE VC AT 1000 METERS FROM CAVALAIR AT AN AZIMUTH OF 30 DEGREES		
31	1025		RECON PLAT: REPT 1 COMPANY OF VC AT COORD 950050		
32	1030		RECON PLAT: REPT 1 POW CAPTURED		
33	1045		RECON PLAT: REPT 2 POW CAPTURED, NOW HAS A TOTAL OF 3		
34	1050		RECON PLAT: REPT HAS 1 CAS WITH A SUCKING SHOOT WOUND		
35	1055		RECON PLAT: REPT HAS 1 CAS WOUNDED IN LEG (RTO WHO CONTINUES TO OPERATE RADIO)		
36	1100		RECON PLAT: ELEM NOW HAS A TOTAL OF 8 POW'S 4 EN KIA		
37	1110		D CO: 1 SQD SENT TO REINF RECON PLAT		
38	1115		RECON PLAT: IN CONTACT WITH UNK NUMBER OF VC		
39	1130		RECON PLAT: REPT 4 ENEMY KIA AND 12 PCW'S		
40	1145		LT WARD: 2 KIA AND 1 WIA		
41	1145	1145	LT PARRACK, 2D PLAT, A CO: BRIEFED BY CAPT LINTON ON MISSION		
42	1155		RELIEF ELEM DEPARTED CAVALAIR BASE		
43	1145		LT WARD: REPT NO SMOKE, WILL BUILD FIRE AT EDGE OF LZ		
44	1145		MED EVAC: WILL NOT COME IN BECAUSE OF NO SMOKE		
45	1150		MED EVAC: APPROACHING RECON PLAT AREA		

PED NAME AND GRADE OF OFFICER OR OFFICIAL OH DUTY SIGNATURE

FORM 1594

ORGANIZATION OR INSTALLATION LOCATION   PERIOD COVERED

			FROM		TO	
			HOUR	DATE	HOUR	DATE
S3, 2/8, CAV		FWD CP	0001	04 NOV 65	2400	04 NOV 65

ITEM NO	TIME IN	OUT	INCIDENTS, MESSAGES, ORDERS, ETC	ACTION TAKEN INL
46	1155		MED EVAC: HIT BY FIRE, WILL LEAVE AREA AND RETURN	
47	1200		RECON AND AT PLAT: MET AUTOMATIC FIRE STILL IN AREA. CAPT LINTON INSTRUCTIONS WERE: (1) KEEP RADIO WITH LT WARD AND (2) KEEP CONTACT WITH VC	
48	1200		RECON PLAT: CAS REPT IS SGT COFFEY KIA, PFC HEMILL KIA AND PFC PATTERSON WIA (RTO STILL ON RADIO)	
49		1200	BDE: SIT REP	
50		1217	CAPT BERNNETT: RELAY TO BDE THAT AT COORD EP8049. RECON PLAT ENGAGED UNK AMOUNT OF VC'S. THEY HAVE BEEN REINF BY 2D PLAT OF A CO. AN ADDITIONAL PLAT FROM CO A WILL IN APPROX 60 MIN LEAVE TO ALSO REINF THE RECON PLAT. THIS LEAVES ONE PLAT OF A CO SECURITY PZ PARIS	
51	1236		RECON PLAT: REPT VC'S ON NW AND NS SIDES	
52	1240		CAPT LINTON TO COL NIX: RECON PLAT IS GETTING REINF WILL HAVE A SWING PSN AND WILL POLICE UP WIA'S AND KIA'S ASAP. WILL BRING POW'S IN	
53	1245		B CO: HAVE CP COORD DP4447 LZ MAKE ROOM FOR 3 SHIPS. WANT BED ROLLS SENT UP	
54	1252		RECON PLAT: PUSHING ENEMY, MOVING WEST TOWARD LZ PARIS	
55	1312		BDE: RELAY TO CA A ELEM, ENEMY SIGHTED AT COORD 087057. NO REPT ON SIZE OR TIRE. MOVING WEST SPOTTED VC'S MOVING INTO WOODS. DUE NORTH OF CAVALAIR 1700 METERS	
56		1321	BDE: REPT THAT A CO MADE CONTACT WITH ENEMY AT 1324. A CO RAN INTO SNIPER FIRE 1317 RECON PLAT AND A CO ARE BEGINNING TO JOIN FORCES 1320. A CO HAS A COUPLE OF WIA'S	
57		1330	BDE: AS OF 1330 HRS RECON PLAT HAS 2 KIA'S AND 3 WIA'S. A CO BETWEEN RECON PLAT AND A CO ELEM	
58	1345		SGT BE THE INTERPRETER FOR THE BN REPT	KIA INFORMED BDE 1350
59	1402		COL NIX: INFORM S4 TO GET M79'S, HAND GRENADES AND SMOKE. COMPANY BASIC LOADS	

PED NAME AND GRADE OF OFFICER OR OFFICIAL OH DUTY SIGNATURE

FORM 1594

ORGANIZATION OR INSTALLATION LOCATION PERIOD COVERED

		FROM		TO	
		HOUR	DATE	HOUR	DATE
S3, 2/8, CAV	FWD CP	0001	04 NOV 65	2400	04 NOV 65

ITEM NO	TIME IN	OUT	INCIDENTS, MESSAGES, ORDERS, ETC	ACTION TAKEN	INL
			LESS 81MM AMMO		
60			BDE: RECON PLAT HAS 2 KIA'S, 4 WIA'S AND THE A CO		
			ELEM HAS 4 WIA'S. SVT BE WAS KIA VC'S ARE 9 KIA		
			AND 5 WIA AND 18 PCW'S		
61			CAPT JORNER: NEED 1 BASIC LOAD AND 2 MULES TO THIS LOC		
62			COL NIX: WANTS TO KNOW WHO HAD THE RED SMOKE		
63			CO B: HAVE LZ FOR 4 BIRDS, CAN MAKE BIGGER FOR 6 BIRDS		
64			CO D: HAS 4 KIA'S AND 5 WIA'S. EVERYTIME THEY TRY TO MOVE THEY GET HIT A SNIPER FIRE		
65	1508		CO D: 26 ELEM HAS 1/3 OF ELEM PINNED DOWN. VC HAS CO (-) SIZE FORCE		
66	1509		CO B: HAS LZ FOR 6 BIRDS NOW		
67	1512		FWD CF: HAS 1 MULE ON THE WAY		
68	1515		MAJ BACHMEN TO CAPT JOYNER: PICK UP ONE ELEM OF C CO		
69	1520		CO D: REPT 1ST ELEM 3 KIA'S, 6 WIA'S AND A CO ELEM HAS 4 KIA'S AND 5 WIA'S 70 REAR CP: HAS INTERPTER BACK IN THERE LOC, WILL BEND HIM OUT WHEN CAN		
71	1530		CO D: REPT THAT ONE PLAT HAS 50% CAS. ELEM FROM CO A WAS HIT BY FRIENDLY FORCES		
72	1535		CO A: HAS 5 KIA'S AND 12 WIA'S AT THIS TIME		
73		1558	CAPT JOYNER TO COL NIX: ASKED PERMISSION TO BURN VILLAGE	COL NIX SAID GO FOR BROKE	
74	1600		C CO: ORDERED BY MAJ BACHMAN TO CLOSE INTO THIS AREA		
75	1610		C CO: 1ST ELEM ARRIVED CP		
76	1620		C CO: 2D ELEM ARRIVED CP		
77	1625		C CO: 3D ELEM ARRIVED CP		
78	1700		ENGER ELEM: CLOSED INTO THIS AREA		
79	1725		D CO:AND A CO ELEM: DD CO 3 KIA'S AND 7 WIA'S. A CO 8 KIA'S AND 12 WIA'S		

PED NAME AND GRADE OF OFFICER OR OFFICIAL OH DUTY SIGNATURE

FORM 1594

ORGANIZATION OR INSTALLATION   LOCATION   PERIOD COVERED

			FROM		TO	
			HOUR	DATE	HOUR	DATE
S3, 2/8, CAV		FWD CP	0001	04 NOV 65	2400	04 NOV 65

ITEM NO	TIME IN	TIME OUT	INCIDENTS, MESSAGES, ORDERS, ETC	ACTION TAKEN	INL
80	2045		C CO: HAVE 12 BODIES COLD, THEY ARE OURS. SHOULD WE TAKE THEM WITH USE		
81	2135		MAJ BACHMAN WANTED TO KNOW WHAT HIS ETA AT THIS LOC. ANS: UNK AT THIS TIME		
82	2137		A CO: HAVE MEN WITH A CRUSHED LEG, HE IS IN A SPLINT AND HAS RECEIVED MORPHINE		
83	2148		MAN CLOSED INTO THIS AREA		
84			MEDIVAC SENT 1 CHOPPER TO CAVALAIR. HAVE 1 PATIENT WITH SERIOUS LEG INJURY. LZ LIGHTED AND SECURE, COORD DEP7137		
85	2227		MEDIVAC EVACUATED PATIENT		
86		2300	BDE: SIT REP		
87		2400	BDE: SIT REP		
88			JOURNAL CLOSED 042400 NOV 65		

PED NAME AND GRADE OF OFFICER OR OFFICIAL OH DUTY SIGNATURE

FORM 1594

ORGANIZATION OR INSTALLATION LOCATION   PERIOD COVERED

		FROM		TO	
		HOUR	DATE	HOUR	DATE

S3, 2/8, CAV FWD CP BATTALION HEADQUARTERS   0001   04 NOV 65   2400   04 NOV 65
YA201842

ITEM NO	TIME IN	TIME OUT	INCIDENTS, MESSAGES, ORDERS, ETC	ACTION TAKEN	INL
1	0001	0015	JOURNAL OPENED 040001 NOV 65		
2	0045	0015	CONT TO DEF ASSIGNED SECTOR NEG EN CONTACT	J	ELW
3		0205	BDE: SIT REP NEG.	J	ELW
4	0220		BDE: MAG FR BDE 6 TO 2/8 CO, OP NOMMITTMENTS PRECLUDE THIS UNIT FROM GETTING LIFT SUPPORT AT 1ST LIGHT. NO ETS TIME WHEN THEY WILL BE AVAILABLE.	FWD CP 0225	CHW
5	0326		BDE: 2/6 WILL NOT GET AIR LIFT AS PLANNED. BDE CO WILL INFORM BN CO WHEN HE KNOWS FOR SURE.	FWD CP: 0328	
6	0330		BDE: TOC SHIP CONFIRMED, HOWEVER, THE OH-13 IS UNK AT THIS TIME	FWD CP: 0332	
7	0350		FWD CP: TELL S4 HE ISN'T GETTING ANY SHIPS. IF HE HAS ANYTHING TO COME OUT SEND IT OUT ON THE TOC SHIP		AMX
8	0422		COL NIX: TELL MAJOR CARROLL TO GET 2 CH-13 REPT AT FIRST LIGHT TO CAVALLAIR. THEY WILL BE USED TO SHUTTLE RATIONS	NOTIFIED MAJ CARROLL 0425	AMX
9	0425		BDE 6 TO COL NIX: SITUATION AT 1/9 CAV LOC REQUIRES THE HELP OF 1/3 ELEM. THE SAME LOC THAT ONE OF 1/8 UNITS WAS MOVED TO AT 2300 HR. 2 BIRDS DOWN (DO NOT KNOW REASON AT THIS TIME). AMBUSH AT HIS LOC ENCOUNTERED SOME VC. EVAC OF CAS IS TAKING PLACE. AMBUSH SITE ENP4043 (UNIT WAS PULLED BACK TO BL 90 N. 7 S.). MSN: MOVE C CO TO LZ SO THAT 2/19 ARTY CAN MOVE IN THERE AT FIRST LIGHT. INFORM BDE 6 AND HE WILL MOVE AND LEAD 2/19 TO THE LZ	MESSSAGED RELAYED BY THIS STATION	
10	0515		BDE: PICKED UP ECHO CODE AND SERIAL PHOTOS		AMX
11	0547		MAJ HALL: YOU HAVE 1 OH-1	NOTIFIED MAJ	AMX

ORGANIZATION OR INSTALLATION LOCATION

			PERIOD COVERED			
			FROM		TO	
			HOUR	DATE	HOUR	DATE

S3, 2/8, CAV FWD CP BATTALION HEADQUARTERS   0001 04 NOV 65 2400 04 NOV 65
YA201842

ITEM NO	TIME IN	OUT	INCIDENTS, MESSAGES, ORDERS, ETC	ACTION TAKEN	INL
12	0800		CAP0T KELLY: YOUR TOC SHIP ARRIVED IN THE BDE AREA AND WAS TOLD REPT TO LT SAWCZYN, BYT INSTEAD MAJ CARROLL TOLD IT TO LEAD RATIONS, WHICH WAS AT 0630. IT DID NOT DEPART THIS LOC UNTIL 0735 FOR THE FWD CP LOC		AM
13	0800		COL NIX TO BDE 6: COL NIX IS OPERATING ON FREQ 281 UHF: ORIGINALLY SENT IN CLEAR BY CAPT BATTS	RELAYED BY THIS STATION	AM
14	0825		CAPT SLIFER TO MAJOR BACHMAN: A COORD 950065. 25-30 VC. POSSIBLY MORE MOVING N TO S. ALONG TRAIL WHERE TWO STREAMS FORK.	MONITORED BY THIS STATION	AM
15	0945		BDE 3 TO MAJ BACHMAN: YOUR C CO ELEM GUARDING 2/19 ARTY IS ATTACHED IMMEDIATELY TO 1/8. REQ C CO COME UP ON 1/8 FREQ.	RELAYED BY THIS STATION: NOTIFIED FWD CP 0950	AM
16	0950	0955	BDE 65: REQ LOC OF CO B ELEM, BDE 65: INFORMED CO B CLOSED PSN AMY (UP4048) AT 0950		AM
17	1010		4 OH-13 ARRIVAL AT S3 AND WAS SENT OUT TO CAVALAIR	RELAYED TO FWD CP	FT
18	1030		FWD CP: 1 VC CPTD 1000 METERS FR CAV ON AZ.30 DEG. ALSO ENCOUNTERED SUSPECT 1 VC CO 950050. ARTY FIRE REQT, WILL COMIT ELM OF RT.	BDE: 1035	CHW
19	1040		CO B: MONITOR RECON AND KEEP ABREAST. WORK W & S OUT OF AMY. ET AT CAV SEND TO RECON, THEY WILL COME		CHW
20	1050		CO C: UNDER OP CTL OF CO D		CHW
21	1115		RCN: HAVE 8 VC PW AND 1 US WIA W/ SUCKING CHEST WOUND. AM STILL ENGAGED AND PIN DOWNED.		CHW
22	1130		HAVE 2 US WOUNDED NOW, 1 SUCKING CHEST AND RCN ONE W/4 RD IN LEG. 4 VC KIA AND 12 VCC. AM STILL PIN DOWN. S3 COMITTED 12 MEN UNDER CMD OF Co D XO TO THE S OF ENGAGEMENT AS REING.		CHW
23		1210	BDE: RON SIT REPT: 12 VC PW, 4 VC KIA, US CAS 1 WIA, 2 KIA. STILL ENGAGED, 1 ELM OF EA CO B & C HAVE BEEN COMMITTED.		
24	1230		COL NIX: AT COORD 980049 RECON PLAT IS IN CONTACT WITH ENEMY. THEY ARE BEING REINF.	FWD TO BDE 1235	AM

ORGANIZATION OR INSTALLATION LOCATION   PERIOD COVERED

		FROM		TO	
		HOUR	DATE	HOUR	DATE
S3, 2/8, CAV FWD CP BATTALION HEADQUARTERS YA201842		0001	04 NOV 65	2400	04 NOV 65

ITEM NO	TIME IN	OUT	INCIDENTS, MESSAGES, ORDERS, ETC	ACTION TAKEN	INL
			BY 1 PLAT FROM CO A. 1 PLAT IS SECURING LZ PARIS FROM CO A. AN ADDITIONAL PLAT FROM CO A IS ALSO IN THE PROCESS OF REINF THE RECON PLAT.		
25	1310		BDE: GP VC MOVING WEST FR COORD 087057 SIZE AND TIME NOT GIVEN. TIME 1255	FWD CP: 1310	
26	1400		FWD CP: SGT BE KIA AT 1300 HRS.		HLH
27	1406		COL NIX: REQ S4 ASSEMBLE BASIC LOAD FOR 1 CO LESS 81MM TO INCL M-79 HAD AND SIKE GREN LIFT INCOUND IN 10 MIN.	INFORMED S4.	HLH
28	1459		BDE: THE 1500 HR STAFF MEETING CANCELLED		HLH
29	1525		COL NIX: WANTS AS MANY MEDICS AS POSSIBLE ROUNDED UP AND HE WILL PICK THEM UP.	MED PLAT NOTIFIED	HLH
30	1534		BDE: CO C ATTACHED TO 1/8.		HLH
31	1540		CAPT JOYNER: ARTY DROPPED IN ON A CO AND THEY HAVE 60 CASUALITIES.		HLH
32	1535		LATE ENTRY: MEDICS SENT OUT TO FWD CP.		HLH
33	1515		LATE ENTRY: PICKED UP NEW INTERPRETER FR BDE (SGT TRACH)		HLH
34	1552		FWD CP: CASUALTY EST APPEARS TO BE QUITE A BIT LESS.		HLH
35	1559		FWD CP: CO C RELEASED FR ATCHMT TO 1/8 AND RETURNED TO PSN CAVALIR.		HLH
36		1700	BDE: REQ EXT ON TIME TO TURN IN DAILY SITREP, APPROVED BY CAPT FOREMAN.		HLH
37	1721		FWD CP: 1 HALF OF CO C HAS CLOSED IN CAVALAIR AT 1625 HRS	BDE NOTIFIED 1725	HLH
38	1728		COL NIX: CO D HAS 3 EM KIA, 7 EM WIA AND A CO HAS 8 EM KIA, 12 EM WIA.	BDE NOTIFIED 1729	HLH
39	1838		FWD CP: CO C IS WEST OF CO A PSN. THEY HAVE NOT MADE CONTACT W/ CO A ELEM YET.		HLH
40		1840	BDE: GET THE WOUNDED OUT ON CHINNOKS OR THEY WILL NEVER GET THEM OUT.	RELAYED TO FWD CP	HLH
41	1840		FWD CP: ALL THE CAS HAS BEEN EVACUATED.	BDE NOTIFIED 1841	HLH
42	1855		BDE: S4 CAN PICK UP ICE ANY ODD DAY AT PLEIKU	S4 INFORMED 1856	HLH
43	1900		BDE: PICK UP MEN AT BDE AND BRING HIM TO THIS LOC AT MEDIC AID STA	DISPATCHED HQ-6	HLH

TYPED SIGNATURE

ORGANIZATION OR INSTALLATION LOCATION   PERIOD COVERED

		FROM		TO	
		HOUR	DATE	HOUR	DATE
S3, 2/8, CAV FWD CP BATTALION HEADQUARTERS YA201842		0001	04 NOV 65	2400	04 NOV 65

ITEM NO	TIME IN	OUT	INCIDENTS, MESSAGES, ORDERS, ETC	ACTION TAKEN	INL
44	1945		JOURNAL AND NOTES RECEIVED AT THIS TIME.	J	ELW
45	2015		CONTACT HAD BEEN BROKEN AT 16 HOURS	T,BOE	ELW
46	2350		BN XO: <u>EN CASUALITY REP</u> A CO 7 KIA (BC)	BDE NOTI-FIED	ELW
			D CO- 5 VCC D CO 15 KIA (BC)	050010NOV	
			B CO- 7-10 WIA B CO 5 KIA (BC)		
			D CO- 30 WAI RESULTS OF ARTY FIRE 30-35		
			A CO 5 KIA 15 WIA TAC AIR 20		
			D CO 3 KIA 3 WIA US CAS		
			ATTACHED ELEMENTS: RRU 2 KIA, 1 WIA		
			ARVN: 1 KIA (INTERPERTER)	J	ELW
47		2400	JOURNAL CLOSED 042400 NOV 65		

TYPED SIGNITURE

Appendix III
After Action Reports

After the completion of every combat operation, the Alpha Company Commander was required to prepare an after-action report describing the unit's activities during the recently completed mission. These reports would also normally include a summary of the action, lessons learned, and recommendations for changes in tactics and administrative and logistical support. The after-action report is considered to be the army's official immediate history of the events that had occurred. In writing *Honor and Courage*, the authors found these reports to be invaluable in recalling events that occured 40 years ago and enabled us to prepare accurate and realistic descriptions of Alpha Company in combat. The after-action reports in this appendix were prepared by 1st Lieutenant Erle Taylor, Captain Thomas Forman, and Captain David Bouton. They cover the period from early February 1966 through late summer 1966.

COMPANY "A"
2D BATTALION (AIRBORNE) 8TH CAVALRY
1ST CAVALRY DIVISION (AIRMOBILE)
APO San Francisco, California 96490

7 March 1966

SUBJECT: After Action Report (18 February 1966 to
         25 February 1966)

TO: Commanding Officer
2nd Battalion (Abn), 8th Cavalry
1st Cavalry Division (Air)
APO U.S. Forces 96490

    1. On the morning of 18 February 1966, Company
A, 2nd Battalion (Airborne), 8th Cavalry, was air
lifted from Mustang Landing Zone to Landing Zone
BIRD vicinity coord BR 745889. This unit took up
defensive positions around the eastern perimeter
negative enemy contact.

    2. On the morning of 19 February 1966 at 1000
hours the unit moved overland to establish a blocking position and company patrol base vicinity coordinates BR 765783. After establishing this position
at approximately 1500 hours several small reconnaissance patrols moved to the east and south. Negative
contact on the southern route, however the Pony Team
to the east discovered many fresh bunkers and three
dead Viet Cong in the village to the east. One
squad sized ambush was established on a trail to the
Northeast of the village, an done platoon sized
ambush to the trail positioned on the southern part,
vicinity cord 768780. Negative contact that night.
However at 0700 hours on the morning of the 18th
hour Viet Cong one armed with a machine gun walked
up on the ambush but spotted it at a distance of
approximately 75 meters. As the Viet Cong turned to
run to the coast (the direction from which they had

come), the ambush took them under fire observing two
of the enemy falling. No bodies were recovered,
however one Viet Cong returned at 0730 hours to give
himself up, he was tagged and evacuated that day.

3.   The Pony Team returned to the eastern side
of the village to establish an eastern block for the
remaining Viet cong. They were followed by the 3rd
Platoon which moved to the south with the 1st
Platoon, the ambush unit, blocking on the south.
The Pony Team was taken under automatic rifle fire
but upon their return of fire they received no more
rounds and were unable to locate the sniper.
Negative contact the rest of the day. An ambush was
established by the 2nd Platoon at coordinates BR
767781 that night but had negative contact.

4.   On 21 February 1966 at 0900 hrs Company A,
2nd Battalion (Airborne), 8th Cavalry, began search
and destroy operations sweeping to the south the
west on coordinates BR 738771. The unit had negative contact on its move and established a company
block to the northeast of objective FLOWER (Mill
342) with an ambush at coordinates BR 734768 with
negative contact.

5.   On 22 February 1966 at 0630 hours the unit
crossed the Nhe Lan river under a heavy ground fog
to seize the eastern portion of objective this was
accomplished at 1230 hours with negative contact.
At 1400 hrs the unit proceeded down the north western slope of the hill to a pick up zone vicinity
coordinates BR 716764. As the aircraft approached
the Pickup Zone they received fire from the village
500 meters to the west of the Pickup Zone. Company
A, 2nd Battalion (Airborne), 8th Cavalry sweep from
northeast to southwest through the village after an
artillery preparation, finding many bunkers and tun-
nels but no contact. The unit returned to the
Pickup zone and closed into position BIRD at 1930

hours taking the eastern section of the defensive
perimeter.

     6. On 23 February 1966, Company A, 2nd
Battalion (Airborne), 8th Cavalry, conducted search
and destroy operation concurrent with Company D, 2nd
Battalion (Airborne), 8th Cavalry, form BIRD, up the
western side of the river to cord BN 757827. At
1300 hours the 3rd Platoon received sniper fire from
coordinates BR 754839. Company A (-) deployed
across the rice paddies to the north with the 2nd
Platoon on line and the Mortar Platoon supporting by
fire. After moving 200 meters across the open paddies the unit was taken under intense small arms
fire from three locations cord BR 777836, 776839,
and 773840. Mortar and Artillery fire was called on
these areas and the units advanced under the bar-
rages. The northern tree line was seized but with
negative contact. The unit then received fire from
its left flank cord BR 765837. Fire was brought and
the unit deployed to this area finding no one. The
unit then began working to the northwest sweeping
the village and tree line and continually drawing
fire. The unit finally deployed under suppressing
fires to Hoi Nhon (3) vicinity cord BR 752841. The
only person found was one old man who said that
there had been 40 to 50 Viet Cong along the tree
line continually with drawing to the northwest and
delaying against the company as it advanced.
Contact had been broken and the unit proceeded back
toward its Pickup Zone BR 770828. However as the
element was about 200 meters short of the friendly
tree line to the south it was again brought under
fire from all areas previously mentioned. This fire
was very accurate and intense, Artillery, ARA,
Mortar fire and small arms fire was delivered
against these positions but to no avail. The Recon
Platoon of Company D, 2nd Battalion (Airborne), 8th
Cavalry, deployed to the right flank of the unit in
and to roll the enemy's flank. The enemy fire

became very intense even though superior fire was brought against it, it continued to inflict casual- ties. The Mortar Platoon then smoked the objective area with white phosphorus and enemy fire ceased allowing the units to break contact and evacuate the wounded. Company A then covered the withdrawal of Company D to the friendly tree line. The unit was extracted to BIRD closing at 2000 hours. Results of action were seven friendly WIA and six enemy KIA (estimated).

7. At 0900 hours on 24 February 1966, Company A, 2nd Battalion (Airborne), 8th Cavalry, made an Air Assault onto the hill top of hill #424 cord 879779 and began search and clear operation to cord 853793 with Comp0any C, 2nd Battalion (Airborne), 8th Cavalry on its left. At 1400 hours the 2nd Platoon on the left flank made contact with estimat- ed Viet Cong Squad at 859795. In the fire fight 2 Viet Cong were captured along with 5 ruck sacks, assorted documents, and a 7.62 mm machine gun with carriage and ammo. The unit then proceeded with two platoons up and one back to cord BR 859998 when the 2nd Platoon again made contact with one Viet Cong but lost him on the western slope of the hill. In the mean time voices had been heard on the right flank to the crest of the hill. The 3rd Platoon assaulted the hill from the northwest with the 1st Platoon blocking on the southwest. Five Viet Cong were killed and assorted gear, documents, ammo, 81 mm shells, and one 7.62 machine gun w/carriage was captured. The unit reorganized started moving to cord BR 859800 where the left flank and point were brought under intense sniper, machinegun and recoi- less rifle fire from hidden Viet Cong position. The point and several other men were immediately killed, the 2nd Platoon pinned down. The CO's order was for the right flank platoon to sweep to the enemy's left flank and rear and the 2nd Platoon to begin crawling forward. The 3rd Platoon began its sweep but as the

2nd Platoon began crawling several more men were hit
and the Company Commander and his RTO were killed by
a sniper at very close range, (estimated 20 - 30
meters). The 3rd Platoon was there in the rear of
the enemy but masking the fires of the other elements. The 3rd Platoon was ordered to hault and lay
down in order to attempt to bring superior fire on
the enemy. The trees were sprayed with one Viet
Cong, KIA definitely observed, and hand grenades
thrown, artillery and M-79 fire were masked due to
the close contact, heavy under brush and placement
friend by units with the 2nd Platoon in front of the
enemy and 3rd Platoon to his rear, all within 50
meters of each other. The 3rd Platoon began its
advance again, hitting 5 Viet Cong and running then
toward the 2nd Platoon. One was definitely WIA and
later captured. The 3rd and 2nd Platoon linked up
but missed the sniper which hid the front of the 3rd
Platoon and the command group pinned down. The
units then threw ten to twenty smoke grenades in an
attempt. The enemy fire did not cease however it
was so inaccurate that the unit were able to accomplish this without taking any more casualties. The
2nd and 3rd Platoons withdrew about 75 meters
through the 1st Platoon who established the security. Company A, then went into a perimeter as did
Company C arrived on the right flank and swept
through the enemy positions which had been abandoned
by this time. Company A and Company C then moved
150 meters to the northeast establishing a perimeter
and cutting a one ship Landing Zone to evacuate the
wounded and take resupply. The dead, gear, and captured material were evacuated on the morning of the
25th February 1966. Results of action: 3 WIA and 6
KIA friendly, 1 KIA enemy (BC) estimated 6 enemy
KIA.

                              ERLE A TAYLOR
                              1st Lt, Infantry
                              Executive Officer

COMPANY "A"

2D BATTALION (AIRBORNE) 8TH CAVALRY
1ST CAVALRY DIVISION (AIRMOBILE)
APO San Francisco, California 96490

7 March 1966

SUBJECT: After Action Report (25 February 1966 to
5 March 1966)

TO: Commanding Officer
2nd Battalion (Abn), 8th Cavalry
1st Cavalry Division (Air)
APO U.S. Forces 96490

At approximately 1000 hours, 25 February 1966, I assumed command of Company A, 2nd Battalion (Airborne), 8th Cavalry, vicinity coordinates BR 860788. At 1130 hours, Company A swept downhill to the southwest to and closed Company B, 2nd Battalion (Airborne), 8th Cavalry position at approximately 1300 hours, vicinity BR 855784.

Our next mission was to block the enemy escape route, vicinity the SADDLE at BR 867809. At 1400 hours, the Company conducted an air assault on a landing zone, vicinity BR 865823 and moved south along the ridgeline to the objective area, closing at dark. We established a blocking position covering the entire main and side trails in the SADDLE, and placed a platoon size ambush at BR 868811.

The next day, 26 February 1966, I decided to move the company down on the eastern side of the SADDLE to vicinity coordinates BR 868807, in order to establish a new and better sited ambush position. This new ambush position was secured at 1100 hours. At 1500 hours I was ordered to occupy the SADDLE again and at 1600 hours the Company was re-established in a blocking position in the SADDLE, and one platoon established an ambush at BR 873806 for the night. During the night one Viet Cong surrendered to the ambush force. He was armed with a light machine gun.

On 27 February 1966, I was given the mission to find and
capture a suspected enemy hospital somewhere in the ravine,
vicinity BR 862813. In order to cover a larger area I moved
one platoon down the ravine on the southwest slope and
started moving the Company (-) down the main ridgeline above
the ravine. At 1300 hours I discovered that the Company was
moving too far to the southwest, so I began movement back to
the North to get back into the area of the suspected hospital. Just prior to this the lead platoon (2nd) spotted 2
Viet Cong that appeared to be getting ready to climb a tree.
They opened fire and killed one, and the other escaped.
Shortly after this we spotted another Viet Cong and fired on
him, missed, and then tried to run him down, to no avail. We
then began to move north, following a small but recently
used trail and at approximately 1500 hours the point squad
was fired upon by one sniper, and at least one or possibly
two machine guns located at vicinity BR 358812. The lead
platoon returned fire and Lt. Stango began to maneuver part
of his platoon. At this time, I was contacted by a scout
ship of the 1/9 Cav, (that is a rocket ship available for
support). We threw smoke and I directed the 1/9 Cav rocket
ship to fire into the Viet Cong firing position. The 1/9 Cav
put their rockets dead into the area from which we received
the fire. Following this the Artillery Forward Observer
called in and directed the fire of two AAA ships. After that
we began to maneuver around to our right in order to outflank the enemy positions while the Forward Observer called
in 105 Artillery fire. While maneuvering around to the
right, the 1st Platoon discovered the hospital area. At this
time I moved the remainder of the company to the hospital
area. It was a large area, so I had the 1st and 2nd Platoons
spread out on line and move forward and up the hill to
search the area out, and had the 3rd Platoon establish rear
and flank security. As the 1st Platoon moved up the hill
they were suddenly fired upon from well-concealed bunkers
approximately 20 to 40 meters to their front. The enemy
force estimated to be at approximately 20 to 30 meters, were
personnel armed with two machine guns and rifles, and were
also throwing dozens of concussions type hand grenades. Upon

recommendation from Lt. Stango who could see the enemy position, I began to maneuver the 3rd Platoon around to his left and the 2nd Platoon right in order to get the 3rd Platoon behind and on the flank to the enemy. As the 3rd Platoon moved around to the right they began receiving a heavy volume of fire from more concealed bunkers on our right flank. At this time I called for a CS grenade drop, which arrived between 1730 and 1800 hours. The CS grenades and our own small area fire kept the enemy fire down to a minimum. Due to the lateness of the day and the fact that I could not make a complete evaluation of the enemy positions, I decided to pull back and establish a perimeter for the night. I moved the 2nd Platoon back across the ravine into a covering position as the 1st and 3rd Platoons disengaged under the cover of smoke. Then as we moved to our next position the Forward Observer called in Artillery fire on the enemy positions. We continued to move to a position approximately 400 meters to the east of the hospital area and secured a small landing zone from which our one wounded man was evacuated by the UH1D at approximately 2230 hours.

The next day, 25 February 1966, we moved back toward the hospital at 0300 hours. En-route the point squad discovered a 12.7 mm A/A MG, complete, and several cans of ammo for the gun. This was brought back to and evacuated from the landing zone by UH1D. When we were in an attack position about 100 meters from the hospital area the Forward Observer started directing fire into the area and we moved forward as the artillery shelled the enemy area. This time we attacked the area from the east and northeast, instead of from the southeast, hoping to hit the enemy on the flank. The 2nd and 3rd Platoons moved forward and started up the hill. The platoons were abreast and well spread out. I had the 1st Platoon stay to the rear for rear and flank security. About 75 meters up the hill on which the enemy had been located the day before, the 3rd Platoon made contact with several well dug in Viet Cong. I was able to observe this platoon as they moved in on the Viet Cong. One squad would place a heavy volume of fire on the Viet Cong positions while another squad moved forward to where they could throw grenades, or fire their M-79's or

LAWs, into the enemy positions. In this manner, the 2nd and
3rd Platoons cleared to the top of the hill, which was about
200 meters from bottom to top. I then moved the 1st Platoon
further south and had the 3rd Platoon move down the side of
the hill where the enemy had been the day before, but they
only found 2 wounded Viet Cong (from an earlier ambush) hiding in the bunker. We discovered about a dozen 1' x 1' x 1-
1/2' tins of medical and surgical equipment, plus a few hundred pounds of miscellaneous clothing. The company killed
(body count) 12 Viet Cong while taking the hill. The company
(-) then moved west down off the hill and closed back to
position CUFF (BR 850812) at 1800 hours. The 2nd Platoon
remained on the hill and prepared a landing zone from which
they and the 2 wounded Viet Cong captives were extracted by
UH1D at 1300 hours.

On 1 March 1966 we made an air assault using 20 UH1D from
CUFF to a landing zone, vicinity BR 934870, and moved north
and then established a blocking position, vicinity BR974888,
to prevent the enemy from escaping by way of the ocean. At
1715 hours we were picked up and moved by UH1D to BR 965870
and established another blocking position facing northeast,
vicinity BR970873. During the night 2 personnel approached
the 2nd Platoon's area in a suspicious manner and were fired
upon, wounded, and captured, and subsequently air evacuated.

On 2 March 1966 the company conducted a search and destroy
operation from the above location to BR 953878 to 953895 to
959901. We found very little evidence of enemy activity in
the area. We were then air lifted back to the previous
night's location and again established a blocking position.

On 3 March 1966 we moved on foot to and established a blocking position facing north from BR 933870 to 943863 to
950868, in order to prevent the escape of the enemy as
Company B and Company C swept toward us from the north. We
had no enemy contact, however. The 3 district representa-
tives asked us to apprehend 2 Vietnamese men in the village
at BR949863 as Viet Cong suspects, which we did and turned
them over to Battalion S-2. At approximately 1630 hours we

were air lifted back to BR955870, where we established a
defense in our assigned portion of the Battalion perimeter.

On 4 March, 1965, Company A conducted an air assault by
"Trooper Ladder" from 4 - CH 47's on the SADDLE at BR931949,
and then conducted a search and destroy operation on the
east side of the ridge line running from BR 927951 to
922975. We found evidence that the entire area had been used
at one time as a large supply storage area, but had not been
used for several months. We made one contact, when 3 Viet
Cong walked into our flank, as we were moving at BR 927951.
One of the Viet Cong attempted to throw a grenade, but our
flank security fired on them first and they fled. The Viet
Cong were pursued, but escaped into extremely thick underbrush and could not be found. We moved to and established a
night defensive position at BR 944984, with an ambush located at 944980.

On 5 March 1966 we were picked up by 3 CH-47's and returned
to the Division Base at An Khe, closing in at 0300 hours.

THOMAS A FORMAN
Captain, Infantry
Commanding

Captain Tom Forman, who proved himself to be a great combat leader
during this action, died in 1993
still a relatively young man. All
the members of A Company who went
up the hill that day will always
remember his skill, courage and
calm leadership under fire.

Thomas Forman
West Point - Class of 1958
07/03/1935 - 11/13/1993

COMPANY "A"

2D BATTALION (AIRBORNE), 8TH CAVALRY

1ST CAVALRY DIVISION (AIRMOBILE)

APO San Francisco, California 96490

7 June 1966

AVCID_E

SUBJECT: After Action Report, Operation Crazy Horse
        (16 May 1966 - 5 June 66)

TO: Commanding Officer
2nd Bn (Abn), 8th Cavalry
1st Cavalry Division (Air)
APO U.S. Forces 96490

1. Summary of Activities: Company A was initially
deployed on 16 May 1966 to PSN COBRA, and was
attached to 1/12th Cav upon arrival. Our first mission was to provide security to the 2/19th Arty Bn
(-) at COBRA. On 17 May we were detached and
returned to 2/8th control, and were airlifted to PSN
SAVOY (800 meters north of COBRA), when the company
provided part of the security for the 2/8th Bn CP
and a 155 How Btry for the next 3 days. On 20 May,
Co A was attached to 1/12th Cav and was committed
to LZ HEREFORD, with the mission to pursue the enemy
forces that had just conducted an attack upon the
Mortar Platoon, of Co C, 1/12th Cav, at LZ HEREFORD.
We were told to pursue along to OXIS, both to the
west. During that night several enemy personal
tried to infiltrate the Co (-) perimeter. Two (2)
enemy were killed, both within five feet of the
perimeter. The pursuit was continued on 21 May
1966, with negative results, and late in the afternoon the company was airlifted to SAVOY and returned
to control of 2/8th Cav. On 23 May 1866, Co A,
conducted an air assault unto LZ CLEMSON, and until

2 June 1966 participated with the Bn blocking mission for most of the period. From 27 May to 30 May
the Company (-) occupied 2 platoon size ambush positions and on 1 - 2 June conducted a search and
clear operation to the NW of CLEMSON. During this
operation 2 different caches of enemy ammunition
were discovered and destroyed. On 2 June the company was airlifted to LZ CRATER and conducted a search
and clear operation from CRATER to HILL 824, 800
meters north of CRATER. From 3 June to 5 June the
company secured LZ CRATER, and on 5 June was the
last unit to be lifter out of CRATER and was
returned to An Khe.

2. Lessons Learned: After leaving LZ HEREFORD in
pursuit of the enemy forces, the Co (-) moved to
the high ground 250 meters to the west and overlooking HEREFORD. Here we discovered firing positions
for two 50 cal MG's, two 57mm RR's, and one 60mm
mortar. All indications were that these firing
positions had been used to support the enemy's
attack on LZ HEREFORD earlier that day. This piece
of high ground was really the key to the proper
defense of HEREFORD, and in enemy hands made HERE-
FORD completely untenable.

3. Recommendations:
          A) The Bn needs a new operations code to
replace the present "White Card".

          B) A special time code would be an added
benefit.

                                        THOMAS A FORMAN
                                      Captain, Infantry
                                            Commanding

COMPANY "A"2D BATTALION (AIRBORNE), 8TH CAVALRY
1ST CAVALRY DIVISION (AIRMOBILE)
APO San Francisco, California 96490

2 August 1966
TO: Commanding Officer
       2d Bn (Abn, 8th Cav
       1st Cav Div (Air)
       ATTN: S-3

FROM: Co, **Co A**, 2d Bn (Abn), 8th Cav
      1st Cav Div (Air)

SUBJECT: After Action Report, Operations Nathan Hale
           and Henry Clay

I.   Operation Nathan Hale (24 June 1966 to 2 July 1966)

     1.   Company, 2d Bn (Abn), 8th Cav departed An Khe
for Tuy Hoa by C-130 on 24 June, closing in the afternoon.   The unit was moved from there to PSN Penny by
CH-47 to secure the northern half of the Battalion Base
area.

     2.   On 25 June the unit air assaulted onto LZ
Quarter and began a sweep in section to the east.
During the night the company was at the perimeter on
objective.   The 1st platoon established an ambush with
negative contact.   Pony 1 was on **OP** and observed the
Viet Cong assembling and moving to the north.

     3.   On 26 June the 1st and 3rd platoons moved to
the valley to the west north west to search for aircraft snipers.   The Co (-) later joined them.   The 1st
platoon drew sniper fire, the 3rd platoon maneuvered to
assist.   The Co (-) joined them at the LZ.   The Bn CO
arrived to brief Co A, 2d Bn (Abn), 8th Cav on the move
to a new area.   The TOC Ship drew sniper fire as it
left and so did the entire element of extraction.

4.   Co **A**, 2d Bn (Abn), 8th Cav assaulted LZ Knife to
secure Bn Base.

5.   On 27 June unit began Eagle Flight operations from
Knife using one platoon at a time. The 3rd platoon was
the first to be deployed to look for suspected enemy
C.P. location with negative results. The 1st platoon
was deployed after extraction of the 3rd platoon. It
located 3 **KIA** and 3 **WIA** civilians from **air** strike. The
1st platoon then was picked up and assaulted to an area
North West of Knife where Pony 1 was in contact. The
1st platoon began receiving heavy sniper fire from the
East and West of their location. The Co (-) was committed and started a sweep with the 3rd platoon blocking to
North and West and the 2nd linking with the 1st to
search. Contact broken by enemy and unit closed at Co
base area. Results 1 VC, 2 VC captured.

   6.   Co A, 2d Bn (Abn), 8th Cav extracted morning
of 28 June to assault to three blocking positions to the
south, June, July and August. No significant activity.

   7.   29 June Co A, 2d Bn (Abn, 8th Cav continued
missions with no significant activity.

   8.   1 July the company moved by foot to the Bn
Base at PSN May to secure the western side of the permi-
ture.

SUBJECT: After Action Report, Operations Nathan Hale and
Henry Clay

   10.On 2 July the unit continued its mission, with
a Bn stand **down**

   11.end of Operation Nathan Hale.

II. Operation Henry Clay

   1. On 3 July co **A**, 2d Bn (Abn), 8th Cav, air
assaulted into LZ Jig and began a search and destroy
mission to the northeast. At 1600 hrs a large (Company
sized) bivouac area was discovered occupied by 3 VC (1
KIA (BC) 1 VIN, and 1 escaped). The company coiled for
a night perimeter with 2 ambushes set out, one squad
sized and one platoon sized.

   2. 4 July the 2nd platoon found a Battalion rest
and training area which was still under construction,
The 1st platoon found evidence that a small force (10-15
men) had just evacuated the area a few days earlier.
The Co (-) continued its sweep to the northeast and
closed PSN George (Bn Base) at dark. The third platoon
established an ambush to the east approximately 1600
meters.

   3. The first and second platoons continued Eagle
flight operations on 5 July to the north of George.
The 3rd platoon was picked up and returned to George to
secure that area.

   4. On 6 July Co A, 2d Bn (Abn), 8th Cav continued to secure George and assaulted to PSN Peter later
in the afternoon to blocking positions. The Co (-) was
at Peter and one platoon each moved 1000 meters to the
east and west respectively. No significant activity.

   5. On 7 and 8 July Co A, 2d Bn (Abn), 8th Cav
continued its mission utilizing extensive patrolling.

6. On 9 July the company assaulted to LZ Redwood
at 0700 hrs with negative contact. The Co (-) conducted search and clear operations along a prominent ridge
to the north. The 3rd platoon moved along the west
flank of the Co in a stream bed. No significant activity recorded.

7. On 10 July Co A, 2d Bn (Abn), 8th Cav continued mission of the previous day extraction **from the bomb**
crater by Ch-47 ladder at 1500. the unit closed at PSN
Pine at 1600 hrs.

8. Co A, 2d Bn (Abn), 8th Cav commences shotgun
patrolling in **assigned** zone of 11 July commencing at
0800 by air landing twelve each six men patrols, three
platoon **CP/OPs** each controlling four patrols, and a Co
(-) **CP/OP**. There was negative enemy contact.

9. Co A, 2d Bn (Abn), 8th Cav continued operation shotgun until 1400 hrs on 13 July. At this time
the unit was extracted to a new company base at LZ
Flattop where the company shared the perimeter with Co
B, 2d Bn (Abn), 8th Cav.

10. The unit was Bn/Bde reserve located at
Flattop on 14 July with negative activity.

11. Co A, 2d Bn (Abn), 8th Cav commenced search
and clear operations north Flattop on 15 July utilizing
A company base and two platoon patrol bases.

12. On 16 July Co A, 2d Bn (Abn), 8th Cav
returned to LZ Flattop by UH-1D to prepare for continuing operations.

SUBJECT: After Action Report, Operations Nathan Hale
            and Henry Clay (Con't)

13.   On 17 July the unit assaulted to LZ ChaCha
Vic, San Bleck, to secure Bn and Artillery Base (B,
2/19th Artillery).   The unit was Bn/Bde reserve force
and conducted only security patrolling around ChaCha.

14.   On 18 July the unit continued to secure
ChaCha with no significant activity.

15.   19 July found Co A, 2d Bn (Abn), 8th Cav (-)
assaulting to LZ Huckle.   The 3rd platoon landed at LZ
Twist and conducted operations in sector.   Two squad
sized patrols landed at LZ Twist and conducted operations in sector.   Two squad sized patrols landed at
Madison for assigned missions.

16.   On 20 July the unit continued its mission in
the area Vic PSN Huckle.

17.   On 21 July the company (-) landed at LZ
Navajo.   The 1st platoon landed at Seminole and conducted operations in sector.   At 1900 hrs that night the
pony team, which was on **OP**, spotted two squads of VC
and a pack animal moving to the northwest away from
Navajo.   Artillery and mortar fire were called with a
result of 3 **KIA (BC)**.

18.   22 July found the company (-) sweeping to the
northwest to search for the escaping VC force, but with
negative contact.   **LZ Apache** was constructed by the company (-) and the remainder of the unit was airlifted in.
The company (-) secured the LZ that night with the 1st
platoon establishing an ambush approximately 1500 meters
to the northwest.

19.   Co A, 2d Bn (Abn), 8th Cav conducted a sweep
to the southwest and closed **LZ Crow** late that afternoon
with no significant action.

20.   The company was airlifted from Crow to LZ
Cherokee (Bn Base) and secured the eastern portion of
the perimeter that night.

21.   The company moved on 25 July to PSN **Valhalla**
(1st Bde Base) securing their assigned sector of the
perimeter.

22.   Co A, 2d Bn (Abn), 8th Cav was attached to
1/9th Cav effective 26 July 0600 hrs.   The 1st and 3rd
platoons were attached to B and C troops 1/9th Cav
respectively.   Negative activity that night.

23.   27 July found the 1st and 3rd platoons conducting Eagle Flight operation with their respective
troops.   The Co (-) remained the reaction force.   At
1200 hrs the unit was **attached** from 1/9th Cav and
attached to 1st Bde Bn for return to Division Base.
The unit (-) moved by C-130 closing Division Base at
1700 hrs.   The 1st platoon closed by CH-47 at 1800 hrs.

David Bouton
Captain, Infantry
Commanding Officer

Charie Black Remembered
1923-1982

Charlie Black
1923-1982

Charlie Black was a simple, straightforward sort of a guy. Charlie was a hometown newspaper reporter In Columbus, Georgia, who covered the military beat for the *Columbus Enquirer*. When the army's new concept of airmobility started taking shape at Ft. Benning, Charlie took notice; after all, it was part of his beat, and it was hometown stuff. Charlie became a familiar face to the men of the 11th Air Assault Division test as they trained and refined the new doctrine of airmobility. When the colors were unfurled for the new 1st Cavalry Division (Airmobile) on July 1, 1965, at Fort Benning, Charlie was there reporting the story. When the Air Cav went to war, Charlie went, too; after all, it was his beat.

Appendix IV
Charlie Black Reports
'Ridge-Running' Mission Begins
With Jump From Helicopter

By CHARLIE BLACK
Enquirer Military Writer

BINH KHE, Vietnam – Captain Roger L. McElroy, commander of Company A, 2nd Battalion (Airborne), 8th Cavalry, is a youthful officer who stands exceedingly proud and tall when he talks about his company.

It is his first command, and he has taken to it with a vast amount of energy and natural talent. I first met McElroy when he was a first lieutenant leading a platoon in the 1st Battalion, 187th Infantry's Charlie Company back in the old days when the 11th Air Assault Division was a controversial item.

Reinforces Beliefs

He was at Fort Stewart in one of the innumerable maneuvers conducted there and was completely dedicated to the idea that men could go into battle in accordance with the new idea for infantry mobility.

Since then, he has had chances to test his beliefs and has reinforced them. I landed with him and his company on top of the mountain at Mang Yang Pass. When they hailed me over to their camp for chow and a promise that they were going to "take off on another ridge-running operation" in the morning, I took them up on it.

First Sergeant John Moore, Lieutenant John C. Miklas, Lieutenant William J. Marr, Lieutenant Guinn D. Parrack, Lieutenant Marty Stango and Lieutenant Erle A. Taylor briefed me on what the morning would bring. The 1st Brigade, commanded by Lieutenant Colonel Harlow Clark, intended to land on top of ridges commanding the rice fields in this area, drive the Viet Cong out of the section, and allow the friendly population, which had fled to refugee camps in protected zones, to harvest the rice.

Rain Stops

"Our part of it starts right here," McElroy said, putting his finger on a map, then pointing through the rain toward a peak in the distance. It quit raining during the night and the early morning brought only fog, mosquitoes, and mud to fill out the discomfort quota of the day. There was every sign that the sun would come out and turn it all into a steam bath by 10 a.m. The operation had great promise of being just what was needed to cause complete physical collapse, but I agreed to climb on a UH1D helicopter with Platoon Sergeant Norman Welch, Staff Sergeant Joseph Dailey, Specialist 4 Billie L. Brandenberg, Specialist 4 Nathan Johnson, and Private First Class George Sykora. Welch, incidentally, is one of the best field NCOs I have met in Vietnam, and has proved to be a remarkable man under the extreme pressures of combat. He is one of the men I have most admired in this country because he is such an absolute master of his job's responsibilities and goes at it with a no-nonsense approach. He is as much of a leader as any single man could be, and his personality outweighs even platoon sergeant stripes in getting things done in the field. The air assault that followed was one of the most unique affairs you could ask for. The "landing zones" were simply little bare spots on the spine of the 2,000-foot-high ridges which the battalion was to secure.

Explains Operation

A crew chief from Lieutenant Colonel Jack Cranford's 227th Assault Helicopter Battalion hurried from one platoon to the other, explaining what was going to happen on top of the mountain. "You guys are going to have to jump out of the chopper," he told the men. "We'll get you as low as we can, but there just isn't room to land up there. When the crew chief says 'go' you don't wait, you jump...and good luck to you." The choppers got off the ground with the usual flapping roar, and the top layer of mud had dried enough in the already hot sun to create a little dust and to cause the men on the ground to whirl around and hide their faces from it. The helicopters then circled and climbed, swept up the valley, crossed the end of the ridge, and came whirling back down, swooping over the tops by following little bare spurs that ran up to the timbered sides of the big hill.

Helicopter Jump Opens Operations

Patch of Grass

At the top was a patch of brown grass spotted with spiny scrub brush and rocks and about 30 feet wide. On one side, a sheer slope dove almost 500 feet to a tangle of jungle, and the same thick mess of thorny vegetation came right up to the top on the side behind. The helicopter hovered at what appeared to be 20 feet altitude and the optimistic crew chief made a motion for us all to unload. "We didn't bring our rappelling ropes!" somebody yelled. "Put this thing down a little!" The pilot finally swooped down to about eight feet, his rotor almost skimming the top of a sapling, and we jumped. I landed off balance, my pack pulling me over. I felt a leg muscle that wouldn't be the same for a couple of days, then landed flat on my back and managed to roll into a rock before going off the long slide into the jungle.

Immense Cloud

I don't really know how the others landed because there was an immense cloud of dust, grass blades, and pebbles, and I had managed to land where I had a worm's-eye view of the bottom of the helicopter a few feet above. It was like looking at an elephant from underneath. The Huey skittered off the slope, and I managed to get up and hobble out of the clear area into the brush just as three more choppers showed up on their way to the little bare spots. Despite the hectic landing, it was the safest I have ever made. It was so obvious that the technique was practically ambush-proof that I didn't even hurry to move into the semicircle put out by Welch, but stopped and looked at the view. It showed the huge rice paddies of the area, the empty villages, the tin roofs of the refugee camps, the barbed wire and ditches of fortified towns and headquarters, and much of the tragedy of this country.

Road Cuts

Red lines across Highway 19 traced out Viet Cong road cuts that were filled in by engineers when the road was reopened. The trails up through empty villages and the crowds moving along Highway 19 in twin lines of white hats and black clothing, with little vehicles in the center, was a good illustration of what this kind of war does to those caught in the middle. Most of those crowds were families who had their homes in the villages where Viet Cong terror and fear of our own actions to clear the VC from the area had made life too risky to be endured. The choppers had landed a full company here before it seemed possible, some having to make two passes to get into the correct position over the tiny little clear places on the ridge top. Not a shot had been fired. Welch kept moving around, and the first thing I knew we were all in a good perimeter, but spaced so that when the command to move came, it could be accomplished without wasted motion. The command came in about 10 minutes. McElroy led us off down the slope first. I thought the downhill part would be easy, but it was actually harder than the uphill sections of the next four or five hours. Every tree and every vine had thorns, it seemed, and the ground beneath the canopy was still mucky and slippery. Rocks caught unwary ankles, and people grabbing at vines or saplings for support speared themselves.

Mangles Thumb

"If I picked a water lily in this county it would have stickers on it six inches long," Taylor told me earnestly after he managed to mangle his thumb on an innocent-appearing twig. He finished the last 40 feet of descent in a manner that plastered the seat of his fatigues with mud and overran most of the platoon ahead of us. The uphill climbs after each ski-slope descent into the little gullies and draws along the mountainside, were grueling and the weather was hot, but they weren't as completely frustrating as the way down. The pace didn't slacken until we came up against a rock structure that I called a cliff and that McElroy spoke of as an "incline," and it became a real mountain-climbing venture. Up at the top I could see the complacent faces of the men of Captain John Martin's Charlie Company, who had landed up there. They kept calling down encouragement.

Big Rock

"Just turn loose and roll up!" somebody yelled as I came to a rock that was too big to hold onto or go around and too slippery to climb over, and I found myself hanging onto crevices in it with my fingertips. I don't know how I finally got extricated, but we all wound up back down in the last gully we had started from, grimly surveying the slope we had just tried. Welch, who had just walked around the whole thing, called to us gently from a nice, smooth trail 100 feet to the left. "Unless you guys just want to, you don't have to climb that. Just come around the path," he said. The Charlie Company comedians who had been watching it all looked disappointed and went back to looking out over the distance.

Last Laugh

I had the pleasure of being there when the word came up that they would go right on back to the peak we had just left, but that they would take a route on the opposite slope that was even brushier and steeper than the way we had come. I said something about last laughs, as I remember. The idea behind all this position switching, McElroy said, was to keep a steady flow of patrols and movement around the ridge top to clear it of any possible sniper resistance and to wind up with the ridge all clearly marked U.S. property. It seemed logical, but it also seemed like more work than I wanted to engage in, since I already understood the technique so thoroughly, so I shook hands all around, complimented them on their mountain-climbing techniques, and caught a chopper back down the ridge. Eight hours of that kind of work is enough for anybody.

Index

To Yearn A Bit

Across the fields of yesterday
They sometimes come to me,

Young men, hard at war;
The boys they used to be.

In my mind, I see their faces
As the memories begin.

I wonder of the men they became,
And of all the might have beens.

Through the years much has passed,
And surely I've grown older.

Yet, I sometimes pause to yearn a bit,
To be once more a soldier.

By Garry Bowles
A Company, 2nd Battalion (Airborne),
8th Cavalry, 1965-1966

5913251R0

Made in the USA
Lexington, KY
26 June 2010